Rich Smith lives in Portreath on the north Cornish coast. He is currently studying for a degree in journalism. His ambition is to become a primary school teacher and continue travelling, as long as US law enforcement doesn't catch up with him.

For more information on Rich Smith, see his website at www.rich-smith.net

YOU CAN GET ARRESTED FOR THAT

RICH SMITH

CORGI BOOKS

TRANSWORLD PUBLISHERS
61–63 Uxbridge Road, London W5 5SA
a division of The Random House Group Ltd
www.booksattransworld.co.uk

YOU CAN GET ARRESTED FOR THAT
A CORGI BOOK: 9780552154062

First published in Great Britain
in 2006 by Bantam Press
a division of Transworld Publishers
Corgi edition published 2007

Addresses for Random House Group Ltd companies outside the UK
can be found at: www.randomhouse.co.uk
The Random House Group Ltd Reg. No. 954009

The Random House Group Ltd makes every effort to ensure that the papers used in its
books are made from trees that have been legally sourced from well-managed and credibly
certified forests. Our paper procurement policy can be found at:
www.randomhouse.co.uk/paper.htm

Typeset in Palatino
Printed and bound in Great Britain by
Cox & Wyman Ltd, Reading, Berkshire.

2 4 6 8 10 9 7 5 3 1

In memory of both my grandmother Jean Ely and Felix

Prologue

I am, by nature, a law-abiding citizen. Before the journey I made to write this book, the only criminal act I had ever committed was a speeding offence on 18 December 2001. The resulting summons meant that the Plymouth Fixed Penalty Commission and I exchanged early Christmas presents – I gave them £60 and they endorsed my driving licence with three points.

The following is an account of what can be achieved when an innocent board game spawns an obsession.

1

Absolute Balderdash

'A wanghee? What the hell is a wanghee?'

The game had reached a critical stage and I delayed my response, playing for time as I put pen to paper to fabricate a definition of the word. Parlour games have never reached Olympic status and the acclaim one receives for winning is fairly minor, but if a civil board game amongst friends could ever host a significant and competitive finish, it was this one – and this final round was crucial.

It was Christmas Day and I had left my friends in the pub in order to play Balderdash with my eleven-year-old neighbour Lewis Ellis and his family. The predictable anticlimactic, turkey-overloaded feeling of the holiday was taking over and I was glad to join a party where the joys of 25 December were still being felt.

Balderdash is basically a board game version of Call My Bluff and it's a favourite yuletide game in the Ellis household. Everyone plays individually and makes up a definition of an obscure word. Your aim is to make your fabrication so credible that your opponents believe it is the real one.

As the game progressed, many of the family members fell by the wayside. Lewis and his brother Danny were strong competitors but their mum and grandparents struggled with the ever-increasing pace of the game and conceivable answers given. By the way she read out each definition, and her general mannerisms throughout play, you could tell that Linda, Lewis's grandmother, was the most in need of help. If her counter's position wasn't a clue as to how poorly she was performing, her countless shrugs of the shoulders, blank stares and almost deliberate failure to understand the rules were a dead giveaway. Each of her responses was either an unwitting 'Oh, the second one' or 'I don't know. I'll go for the same as Lisa'. These answers were always met with an ardent outcry from Lewis, who was starting to become frustrated at his nan's inability to follow play or think for herself. She was in full possession of her faculties, but when it really counted – playing board games – she lacked the relevant qualities required for victory.

Lewis was in total charge. He was the youngest player in the game and also the most competitive, but he wanted to win fairly and didn't go in for the usual indulgence towards youngsters that normally accompanies yuletide parlour games. I respected him for his integrity, and as he was just a point from victory he obviously didn't need any favours. I, on the other hand, was five points from being crowned Balderdash champ and not only required a definition that would fool everybody but also had to guess the true meaning of the word myself – achieve a 'Jackpot', in short. We were at a crucial stage in the game and as Lewis selected a card from the box, magnificently aware that it was a non-scoring round for him, he knew that only a miracle would stop him from claim-ing board-game supremacy when it was my turn to play quizmaster.

'A wanghee . . . a bloody wanghee?' I thought to myself. I wouldn't have worried under normal circumstances but this time my definition had to be a good one. Brilliant, in fact. Good just wouldn't cut it.

'Hurry up!' shouted Lewis, becoming impatient in the build-up to his impending coronation.

'OK, OK. Hang on. I've almost finished,' I replied. I had finished writing and my definition was believ-able. Possible at the very least. I read it back to myself: 'Wanghee: a small South American bird that nests in the fur of other animals.' It sounded good. Very good. As I handed it to Lewis, he read it to himself to check that it was legible and he could pronounce each word. The usual smirk of confirmation that normally followed was not forthcoming and my submission was greeted with a slight shake of the head.

What did that mean?

Lewis had played this game many times before but I was a Balderdash virgin. I'd never had a shake of the head as a response from the boy at any time before and it worried me. Had this been used in a previous game which the members of his family were sure to recollect? Was it *so* stupid that not even Linda was going to choose it, even if it was read second or was the one that Lisa chose?

'A wanghee,' Lewis began. 'Is it . . .' The first four definitions followed, then: '. . . Chinese bamboo used for making canes; or a small South American bird that nests in the fur of other animals?'

God, it sounded even better when accompanied by the other definitions.

'Yep. I've heard of that. It's the South American bird.' There was an air of certainty about Lisa's response. I liked it. She sounded convincing enough to plant a seed of belief in the minds of the others.

'I'll go for that too,' added Cliff, the grandfather.

'Oh, I'll just go with what Lisa said.' It was good to hear Linda's trademark one final time.

Lewis looked concerned.

'It might be the bird one,' said Danny cautiously. He wasn't about to rush into any decision like his family. He was cagey and played the game logically. 'That bird one's yours, isn't it, Rich?' he asked. He paused and waited for a crack in my poker-faced defence. Still, however hard he tried, he couldn't forget the comment his mother had made and in an act of

12

allegiance to her intellect he eventually declared, 'Yeah, I'm going for the bird one too.'

'Well, the bird one does sound tempting,' I said, trying to hide any signs of ownership. 'But the only thing that stops me going for it is the fact that I wrote it,' I added. A toothy grin spread over my already glee-filled face. The hard work had been done – they had all picked my answer. All that was needed now was to select the correct definition from the remaining five.

'It's got to be the bamboo,' I said to Lewis.

It had to be the bamboo. The others were ridiculous entries that I couldn't even remember and it was the only one that made any kind of sense. 'Yeah, I'll go for the bamboo, Lew.'

Lewis didn't say whether I was right or wrong, but the direction of his gaze convinced me I was correct. His long glance at the board, counting the number of squares I'd be moving, was enough of an indication to confirm what I already knew.

'And Rich wins,' came his disappointed drone of congratulation.

'Sorry, mate,' I replied sincerely.

I was sorry. I felt bad about my success. I had not only won the game but snatched triumph from an eleven-year-old's grasp just when he could taste victory – and on Christmas Day of all days. I didn't quite know what to say to cheer him up.

Stuff it.

'WINNER!' I yelled jubilantly at the top of my lungs. 'I can't believe you all fell for it!'

I figured you only get one chance to spoil a young boy's Christmas Day – and I was going to make the most of it. Lewis knew I was only joking anyway.

'Yeah, good game, Rich.' Lewis had recovered from his upsetting defeat very quickly. The boy was competitive, there was no doubt about it, but he was a good sportsman. He knew he'd been beaten by a better man on the day and was pleased that he had come so close to beating his neighbour. A neighbour who was *twice* his age.

We chatted as we packed the game away. I started to flick through the box of cards. A previous answer had intrigued me to such a degree that I found myself searching for similar ones. An obscure word didn't have to be the subject: unknown abbreviations, film titles, people, or, most bemusing of all, completely inane laws might come up as a question. Earlier in the game, I and the entire Ellis family were left to wonder which activity was illegal for divorced women, in Florida, on Sundays. Many suggestions were made but no one was even remotely close to the truth. And for the first time that evening, the real answer was far more ludicrous than any of our manufactured ones.

'It is illegal for a divorced woman to go parachuting on a Sunday.'

What?

Why?

I still didn't believe it.

It simply made no sense. I spent the next few

14

minutes thinking of reasons why such a law existed. Maybe women with failed marriages were heavily frowned upon from a reverent viewpoint in the state of Florida and God didn't want them so close to him up in the clouds – especially on *his* day.

The true explanation was unfathomable, though I was sure there must be some sort of esoteric justification. Come to think of it, the reason didn't bother me so much. What was fascinating to me was the fact that the law existed. The most entertaining country in the world had given me yet another reason to smile.

By the time New Year had passed and 2004 was well under way, I still hadn't forgotten the astonishing discovery I had made on Christmas Day. I wanted to learn more. I wasn't just content in the knowledge that certain people were banned from parachuting in Florida. I was in need of additional information regarding similar laws and was desperate to investigate further. I was hungry for it.

Modern technology has taught us that if you want to find out anything, the Internet will very often disgorge whatever you require. It is the one twentieth-century innovation that has changed the way we search for information and I was sure that I was just a mouse click or two away from laying my unsettled mind to rest.

A simple on-line search for 'stupid American laws' quickly found dumblaws.com, a hilarious if vaguely alarming site filled with examples of these archaic decrees. I clicked on the 'American' option and was treated to a fifty-page, state-by-state guide. I was starting to get excited, and by a website! A site where there wasn't even a hint of nudity. Every page brought new laws and a bigger grin of delight to my face.

In Atlanta, Georgia it is illegal to tie your giraffe to a telephone pole or street lamp; you aren't allowed an ice-cream cone in your back pocket throughout the entire state of Alabama, and it is considered a felony in Arizona if you protect yourself from an intruder with any weapon other than the one the trespasser possessed. I pitied the man who decided to leave a nine-iron under his bed for protection, only to find that his would-be burglar chose to break in with a putter.

God, these were good.

The site was easy to navigate and for each state there was a list of laws that existed throughout and ones that only applied to certain cities. There were literally thousands of examples and I found myself staring at the screen as if not a single moment of my life was being wasted on this notoriously addictive activity.

I began to wonder just who the last person was to break the giraffe-tying law, or indeed if anyone had ever managed it. I reckoned the only way for the ban to be breached was to steal a giraffe from the local zoo first, and I'd like to see someone try to smuggle a mammal that size out through the exit gate under their jumper.

After several pages, I was beginning to focus only on the laws that were either ludicrous or potentially actually enjoyable to break. Spitting on the floor of a church featured heavily but was neither funny nor farcical and I could see good reason for its existence. But there were a few that sounded promising: bowling on the sidewalk was illegal in Chico, California, as was falling asleep in a cheese factory throughout South Dakota.

Could you get arrested for committing these acts? Did the local police even know of their existence? Surely if I was aware that it was against the law to shout 'Oh, boy' in Jonesboro, Georgia, the residents must be too. I wanted to know, I needed to find out and I was now seriously considering going to the States to answer these pressing questions. A little over an hour had passed since I'd discovered an abundance of these laws and now I was thinking of pursuing my investigation further on the grandest of scales.

I decided I would invest in some more research and soon came across a book entitled *The World's Stupidest Laws*, written by an ex-magistrate by the name of David Crombie. I knew that many of the laws which were posted on the Internet might not be true, and if I was going to spend thousands of pounds on some pointless endeavour I might as well get it right. Several of the laws which I saw on dumblaws.com didn't feature in the book but a good many of the funnier ones did and I decided that I would treat the book as my bible – scripture which I would live by throughout my time in the States. If a law appeared within the pages of the book, I would consider it a law; if it didn't I wouldn't. Simple as that.

I am no stranger to pointless endeavours. In June of 2004 I was bet £20 that I wouldn't 'storm' a beach in Normandy on the sixtieth anniversary of the D-Day landings and, with 6 June only an hour and a half away, I drove to Dover, boarded a ferry, had my photo taken whilst on the beach and returned home almost twenty-four hours after I had set off, a total of forty-two hours without sleep. It had cost me £60 to win a third of that amount but the sense of personal achievement I felt more than made up for the financial loss. Sod the sceptics: as far as I was concerned I had accomplished something special.

The travel bug stayed with me for the next week and I decided to nip over to Spain to surprise my neighbours. Their hired villa took six hours to find due to its secluded location in the mountains overlooking the Costa Blanca, but, using nearly every mode of transport available to me from trams and taxis to a free lift with a delightfully generous lady from Portsmouth, I was once again equal to the challenge and enjoyed three nights of free accommodation in picturesque Spanish seclusion with the family's two over-the-moon children and their not-so-happy parents. I was sure that I would pay for the ordeal I had put them through when we all returned home, but as I slowly sipped a refreshing post-swim drink whilst gazing at the rolling green hills of the Costa Blanca I felt victorious, and, although I felt an equal measure of guilt and sympathy towards my neighbours, I knew I had reached a personal high with a view of the mountainous coast as my reward. A little under eight hours had passed since I had set foot on Spanish soil for the first time, clutching a scrap of paper with the name of my destination inscribed on it, but now I was reminiscing fondly about the monumental journey I had made to get there. I was proud of my actions and the bad vibes I had created with my unprepared hosts weren't going to dampen my celebratory spirits.

I needed a companion for a trip of this magnitude. I was now contemplating not only a few law-breakings but a daring crime spree – a journey that would take me from one coast of America to the other in a thrilling two-month adventure. I knew just the man.

Though Luke Bateman and I are best friends, we had only travelled together once before at this stage – a trip that neither of us would ever forget. A drunken arrangement in the pub one night had landed us in the port of Tallinn two weeks later to watch the 2002 Eurovision Song Contest live in the Estonian capital. Neither of us could remember why we decided that visiting a Baltic nation whilst it was hosting a risible talent contest was a good idea, but we were glad that this was the result and we were fully prepared to make the most of the situation. After declining a kind invitation to purchase a Russian passport and gas mask from an Estonian salesman, Bateman and I visited a brothel which masqueraded as a 'strip bar/nightclub' (the flashing neon light above a secluded cottage should have been a big clue but I was still shocked when I realized what kind of place I was in), got drunk with a German photographer and a transvestite, and found our three-day holiday was to be extended to four when we missed our connecting flight to Copenhagen after passing out on a portside beach at five o'clock in the morning. This was the man I needed. Bateman would make a noble accomplice.

The pitch had to be well thought out and elaborately explained. Bateman wasn't just going to agree to an idea like this. I began to think I would be more successful if I plied him with alcohol and then, when he would more or less agree to anything, got him to sign a watertight contract for future ratification to confirm that he did agree to accompany me on my odyssey. As I drove to his house I had the spiel all figured out. I had answers to all his possible questions and any comeback he might present was amply prepared for.

'Hiya, Bateman. All right?' I asked when I arrived.

'Yeah.' He yawned. 'Bit tired, though.'

'I've got a great idea for something for us to do,' I stated proudly. This wasn't anything new for Bateman. Quite often I'd turn up at his house with an absurd agenda for our activities that day.

'Well, I've got to go to the gym at five so we can't be long,' he replied.

'That's OK, I wasn't really thinking about today. This is a bit more long-term.' This was it. No more small talk. It was time to use all my persuasive guile and chicanery to sway my friend. I was ready. 'Um . . . how would you like to go to America some time and break some laws?' That was well put.

'What?' Bateman looked nonplussed.

'There are loads of stupid laws we can break. We could turn it into a road trip . . .' I began to lose my argumentative mien '. . . you know? It'll be great!'

Bateman just laughed. 'Why are we going to do this?'

'Because . . . um . . . I think you and me will have a great time filming it. We could try to get a TV series out of it or something.'

'Yeah. Go on, then. I've got nothing better to do. When we gonna go?'

'Next summer?'

'Yeah. OK.'

That was it? That was all it took? Bateman was in. The trip was beginning to come together nicely. Briefly, I wondered if Guy Fawkes and the rest of the Gunpowder conspirators were as easy to recruit.

The laws began to envelop me in the following months and I began to reveal my plan for a crime spree the following year to friends. My neighbours thought it was a great idea and were happy as long as they featured in the book. Mission accomplished. The invariable response I received, whoever I talked to, young or old, was that it was a great idea. 'Smashing', 'excellent', 'cool'. Were they mad? They all knew what I had done in the past and were quite certain I would be equally successful this time. Not one person I spoke to labelled it 'unrewarding' or 'wasteful'. Everyone agreed it was 'stupid' and 'pointless', but they were obvious features and weren't up for discussion. Everyone believed wholeheartedly in the spree, and in me. If there was ever a doubt in my mind that I was going to do this, it soon disappeared when the consensus amongst friends and well-wishers was more than encouraging. Living vicariously, I suppose.

Bateman and I weren't prepared to attach a giraffe to a lamppost or wait to be attacked by a weapon-wielding intruder, but we found about forty laws that we wanted to break. That was our target. I looked at a map and realized that this was to be a journey of epic proportions. It would take us cross-country from the liberal, laid-back surroundings of San Francisco on America's Pacific coast through the rugged, diverse terrain of mountainous Colorado and Utah, then through the country's Midwest, to the verge of the Atlantic in Florida and South Carolina before we made our way to the culmination of our venture in the north-east, near Boston and Rhode Island. A trip of well over ten thousand miles was laid out before us. To me, the beauty of it all was that the majority of the law-breaking would take place in towns and cities little known to many people – 'small-town America', in fact. I have noticed, from previous experience, that these small, out-of-the-way backwaters of the country are where the true characters live, where the cogs of the country turn, the people are closer and the atmosphere is friendlier, unlike the anonymity of the larger towns.

Once upon a time, the prospect of embarrassment and possible incarceration whilst attempting to break the law would have daunted us, but no longer. Our hearts were set on this journey; our time had arrived. This was our chance to do something admirable and courageous. Something we could be proud of; a tale with which to regale friends and grandchildren alike. Bateman and I were going to America and we were ready for anything.

Or so I thought.

2

Media Mayhem

A good few months had passed and, although the tickets to the States had not yet been purchased, it was clear to Bateman and me that we would spend the majority of the summer of 2005 over there, regardless of the inevitable credit card bills we would amass and the wrath we would incur from our respective employers.

In my mind, the timing was exactly right. Not only was there lots of law-breaking to plan, but there was also the minor technicality of my college course to consider. The first year of my journalism degree would end a month before we left and would give me a clear three months to play with before the course resumed in the autumn.

As any student knows, the relevant coursework has to be accompanied by something no person over the age of fifteen ever wants to think about – work experience. The mere mention of the words injects fear and loathing into the heart of anyone, like me, who has already worked full time for many years and doesn't think too highly of the entire concept. Though I hadn't really explained this to the faculty, I actually wanted to be a teacher and so needed a degree – and journalism college was selected for the sole reason that it was closest to my house. It all seemed like a bit of a waste of time. Besides, how could anything possibly live up to the week's work experience I had served at my local leisure centre a year before my GCSEs? Five days was spent either watching the opening group games of Euro '96 (occasionally checking members' passes) or attempting to avenge my defeat earlier in the week on the badminton court against a highly skilled member of the over-60s badminton club who looked distinctly like Ernie Wise. That was work. Sitting behind a desk watching TV interrupted only by the odd passing fitness fanatic was good enough for me. It was easy, fun and didn't teach me anything I needed to learn in order to aid my future search for employment in the slightest.

Eventually I admitted to myself that sooner or later I would have to comply with the course structure if I was to pass the first year – but I had a plan. Fortunately, I knew someone who could help me out, and without expecting me to do very much.

David Green was the editor of the local edition of our regional newspaper, the *West Briton*. He agreed to take me on for the week and on the Monday warned me how dull I might find the following five days.

'That doesn't bother me, David,' I said sincerely. 'As long as you sign that piece of paper which says I was here, I'll be happy. What shall I do first?' David perused his diary and flicked through randomly assorted Post-it notes and indecipherable scribblings.

'There you go.' He handed me a small scrap of paper. 'Ring this lady, get a quote and write a story about the senior citizens' party she organized.'

David's warning instantly manifested itself into reality. The story I wrote was as thrilling as the quote which accompanied it – 'They had roast beef with all the trimmings and it all went well.' Hold the front page.

As the week progressed, I visited the opening of a factory, made a Mother Goose production sound tenuously exciting in text, and appeared at the media table to witness the monthly Kerrier District Council Planning Committee meeting. I only stayed for the first three hours of the meeting, which eventually lasted a further five. The cogs of local democracy appear to turn at an excruciatingly slow pace.

When I returned to the office on the Wednesday I thought I would enliven the deathly quiet atmosphere of the news room (well, the only room) by regaling David with the story of my proposed trip to the States in the summer. David didn't look as if he was listening and continued to check his copy for clarity and errors. I continued regardless and after explaining everything that was pertinent, sat back and awaited his response. David relaxed into his chair and removed the biro from between his lips.

'You're seriously going to do this?' he asked with a glint of approval in his eye.

'Yeah, why not? Should be fun,' I replied whole-heartedly.

'Well, in that case, I think it'll make a great feature for next week's paper. Can you manage about six hundred words?'

Six hundred words? The senior citizens' party was only allocated fifty – that made me at least twelve times more important than them, I reckoned. As far as the *West Briton* and local newspapers go, this was a scoop.

Then it occurred to me that my name would appear as the reporter. It would look slightly arrogant that someone had composed a story about himself.

'Do I have to put my name as the author, Dave?' I asked cautiously.

'Of course you do. Who else wrote it?'

I decided to reword the original question.

'But does *my* name have to be on it? It's my story so surely I'm entitled to use a pseudonym, aren't I?'

David looked intrigued. 'What kind of name were you thinking of, then?'

'Chris Mardith. It's an anagram of Richard Smith. Clever, hey?' I was certainly proud of it.

In almost no time at all, the name received the thumbs-up, the story was written, a mugshot-style picture had been taken and my week in journalism had come to an end. The five days of 10 a.m. starts, one-hour lunch breaks and 2 p.m. departures had taken their toll and I was glad to leave behind the hectic schedule my week in the media had created and return to my lazy lifestyle.

It wasn't until the following Thursday that I could open the paper and see my story in its entirety, adorning half a page with accompanying picture. Apart from a few shortened quotes, the story was more or less word for word what I had originally written and I was proud of my accomplishment of featuring in a newspaper without having to fall through a window and lacerate my arm as I had done a few years previously. The only reservation I had about the story was the choice of headline the sub-editor had selected. MISSION TO GET ON THE US 'MOST WANTED' LIST didn't really convey the true sentiment of the trip. It wasn't my ambition to feature on the list at all. Breaking silly laws was one thing but in order to rub shoulders with the other nine most ruthless felons in America I would have to knock Robert William Fisher down into eleventh place by committing more heinous crimes than his triple homicide and arson of an occupied building.

A few of my friends commented on the story on the day of issue and I felt a minor celebrity in my little north-coast Cornish village, but I was hardly prepared for the call I received that evening from a man by the name of Sam. Sam worked for the Press Agency in Plymouth and it was his job to scour all the south-west's newspapers for stories in which the nationals might show an interest. I pitied him instantly.

'I'm not promising anything, Richard, but a national or two may pick it up. I really don't know.' Sam seemed very uncertain, but I didn't really care. It was all a bit of a novelty anyway.

'Do you reckon I could make the *Sun*, Sam?' I had always wanted to appear opposite the inside front cover. And it wouldn't be the first time there had been three tits on page three either.

'Just wait and see, Rich.' And with that the conversation ended and it went straight out of my mind.

Friday is always 'Fish 'n' Chips Day'. It's the law. In every job I've ever had, my colleagues have eaten the British culinary delight religiously on that day and I see it as my duty to continue the tradition. The Friday following my newspaper appearance was certainly no exception and I picked up my usual cod and chips and curry sauce on the way home. No sooner had I parked my car and raised the handbrake than my mother rushed out to greet me.

'Thank God you're home. The phone's been manic,' she said, clutching various scraps of paper on which she had kept the messages. 'You'd better eat your dinner quickly. Some are about to call back.'

John Brown of the *Independent*'s was the first of many calls I would end up taking that afternoon. My mobile was similarly busy, and when I first turned it on it reacted violently like a fruit machine writhing in pain. I managed a couple of forkfuls before the phone rang again.

It turned out that my college lecturers, Jacqui Boddington and Mark Benattar, had been taking calls for me all morning. They had already rung my mobile several times (which I was ignoring by now, trying to keep up with the landline) and had finally reached me at home. They had received four calls from radio stations and warned me that they had passed on my number.

My dinner was fed to the dog.

By 5 p.m. that evening, only three hours after returning home from my part-time job, dull data entry, I had spoken to reporters from half a dozen national newspapers and organized telephone interviews with several radio stations. It was as if everyone wanted a piece of me and although I am nearly six foot five it didn't seem as if there was going to be enough of me to go round. Somehow my short and seemingly innocuous article had spawned a media circus and frankly I was a little overwhelmed. And still the calls kept coming. The media were like vultures (nice vultures, the kind that would arrive on time for dinner and not leave the corpse waiting before they picked away at the rotten flesh) and wouldn't leave me alone until they were satisfied with the gatherings of their swoop.

I appeared in the Saturday editions of the *Guardian*, the *Daily Mail*, the *Sun*, the *Daily Telegraph* and *The*

Times, and also featured in the *Cornwall Independent* and the *Western Morning News* the following day. On the Friday and Saturday alone I did live interviews on BBC Radio Five Live, BBC Radio Cornwall, BBC Radio West Midlands, BBC Radio Cambridgeshire, BBC Radio Wales, and I had the privilege of talking to the BBC World Service from one of the Radio Cornwall studios which had been kindly unlocked late on the Saturday night especially for me. The curious appetite of today's media was summed up by the BBC World Service interview, where I received almost twice as much airtime as the previous story on the Rwandan genocide. There was something definitely disconcerting about that.

The other thing that niggled me about the newspaper and radio coverage was their constant comparisons of Bateman and me to Butch Cassidy and the Sundance Kid, Thelma and Louise or, even more alarmingly, Bonnie and Clyde. Let's consider their endings. Butch and Sundance go out 'all guns a-blazing' and inevitably die; Thelma and Louise decide to end it all at the bottom of a cliff; and the police unloaded 167 rounds of ammunition into the car in which Bonnie and Clyde were hiding – fifty entering the fugitives' bodies alone. Hm.

In the week which followed, I featured in Taiwan's *Taipei Times*, India's the *Hindu* and *Reader's Digest* – at least that meant I could reminisce about my American adventure whilst waiting for a doctor's appointment in six years' time. After further radio interviews with

Manchester's Key 103, Beat 102/103 and RTE in Ireland, Australia's 6PR in Perth and 720 ABC, I knew it was only a matter of time before the Americans found out about me and my illicit intentions.

It occurred to me that our relatively innocent holiday was gaining more exposure than I would have liked. The idea was conceived quite spontaneously and surely that was half the fun. If I wasn't careful, I would lose any kind of control over the entire affair and that was something I knew I didn't want. It had already reached the point where the fun trip felt more like a project and the main fear now was that America might not even allow us into the country.

On 3 March I received my first call from across the pond. Someone had read one of the dozen stories that had somehow made their way on to the stateside newsstands.

'Hi,' he started, cheerfully enough. 'My name's Dave O'Brien and I co-host the Wank and O'Brien Show in—'

'Pardon?' I interjected. Surely this was a wind-up. It's a good job I didn't say 'Come again?'

Dave repeated his introduction and, after assuring me that his co-host's name wasn't at all comical in the States, requested an interview with me.

I agreed to be taped for broadcast on their breakfast show the following morning. They invited me to join them in the studio whenever I came through Indianapolis and I was only too happy to agree. There was no way I was going to pass up the opportunity to sit opposite Ed Wank. Once more, I was beginning to look forward to the trip.

The calls and emails continued for a month or two following the news hype and it wasn't until my birthday on 20 March, when not one single call or email intruded, that I felt as if the whole ballyhoo had finally died down. I could return to simply looking forward to being a felon in the USA and planning the route we'd be taking.

A road map, blank A3 printouts of America and the book of laws were laid out on my living room table and a pack of fluorescent highlighting pens that I had bought several years ago was brought into play for the first time. West to east had always been my preferred route but now, with the extensive media coverage I had received in the States, I was seriously considering flying to the Canadian city of Vancouver and crossing a land border where, I hoped, no probing questions would be asked before making my way down to San Francisco.

A few hours and a couple of bottles of wine later I had come up with an ingenious and foolproof plan. Across the road map, I had plotted a series of numbers, each of which corresponded to the specific town and law in question. I could now calculate, almost to the hour, exactly when and where each law-breaking incident would take place. It was very impressive, if I say so myself. A little too impressive, in fact, and when I finally realized that I had created

34

a ridiculously strict itinerary which left no room for chance encounters or lost weekends, it wasn't long before, instead of taking its place on the wall, the plan was torn up and shoved in the bin.

'We'll just fly to San Francisco and take it from there,' I told Bateman the next day.

With glorious hindsight, I accepted that the emphatic wave of attention with which I had been struck had definitely made me more savvy and, in a way, the work experience had taught me a great deal about the power of the media. If I wasn't ready for a trip of this magnitude before, I certainly was now, and no God-fearing southern-state sheriff was going to stand in my way. No cell was going to contain me and my date with destiny. If I could cope with this, I could handle eight weeks in an enclosed space with Bateman. I was ready for America. In my eyes, July couldn't come quickly enough.

3

Not the American Dream Start

Due to its position in the bay, Alcatraz Island dominates any view from the many piers that make up Fisherman's Wharf, the most northerly point of the San Franciscan peninsula. Before the rocky islet became the world's most feared high-security prison, the island was home to nothing more than the odd pelican (*alcatraz* in Spanish). From 1934 and for almost thirty years, the island was home to the likes of Al Capone and Machine Gun Kelly, who resided there with some of the most ruthless criminals in America.

The conditions were inhumane: the darkened cells were no bigger than five feet by nine feet and all inmates were kept in solitary confinement. They weren't allowed to talk to each other, play cards or even read newspapers, and visits were restricted to two hours a month. Nowadays, however, those who go to Alcatraz are only tourists, and the queue that forms at pier 41 every day shows just how much the stringent visiting regulations have changed now that the island welcomes more than 750,000 sightseers every year. All of whom are free to leave.

When you take a tour of the bay, you soon forget the dreaded history of Alcatraz when the sun breaks through the clouds to paint the island's lighthouse a natural gold as the rays find gaps in the towers and suspension lines of the Golden Gate Bridge.

Or so I'm told.

Today as I stand on the wharf, the fog that plagues this part of California is so thick that I can barely make out the rock on which Alcatraz stands. And as for the Golden Gate Bridge, well, my map assures me it's there somewhere. As I turn to face the city, the conditions are merely a little overcast and nothing except the 853-foot TransAmerica Pyramid building is sufficiently high to penetrate the cloud cover. The difference in views is similar to the turning of a postcard.

Although there was no actual law to break on Alcatraz itself I had been hoping that the trip would symbolically begin on the island, which struck me as the most apt of places to begin an American crime spree. However, for obvious reasons, Bateman and I would have to make do with the shores of Fisherman's Wharf, and hope that the scene of some of the inmates' final steps on mainland soil would

shine just a little light of infamy on the starting point
of our felonious adventure.

It was time to retreat to the hotel and regroup.

According to an old city ordinance which has
apparently yet to be repealed, the country's most
liberal city still forbids oral sex – given or received.
Usually, attaining that level of intimacy with a young
lady in only one night would be nigh on impossible
for me, but in America my track record was actually
pretty good.

When I was in Los Angeles in 2002 for my twenty-
first birthday, my friend Chris and I decided to take a
taxi to Hollywood to visit a strip bar. With a name like
Perversion, the club and the night's proceedings were
guaranteed to please and, after arriving slightly early,
Chris and I propped ourselves up at the bar to begin
an evening of drinking. After surprising the barman
with the pace at which we ordered a staggering
number of vodka and Cokes, we looked around to see
if anything was happening. The dance floor which
surrounded the catwalk was beginning to fill with
people but no scantily dressed women yet graced the
raised platform with their presence. As Chris ordered
another couple of vodka and Cokes, now using his
credit card to pay for them, I made a visit to the toilets,
meandering through the crowd which had started to
gather. As I passed each person, rubbing shoulders
with many, I noticed that something just wasn't quite
right but I couldn't put my finger on it. Thinking

nothing more about it and realizing it would come to me eventually, I entered the bathroom and after the necessary business had been taken care of turned and noticed that a gentleman was offering me a towel to save me the complicated procedure of taking one myself.

'Thanks,' I remarked as I took the towel.

'You're brave, aren't you?' he replied.

'Pardon?'

'Dressed like that.'

'Why, what's wrong with it?'

'Nothing. But every Thursday night is Goth night. Didn't you notice everyone else?'

I opened the door slightly and peered back towards the dance floor. The entire building was filled with people with white faces, spiky black hair and long, dark trench coats. I must have been drunker than I thought not to have noticed it earlier. At least as I made my way back to the bar Chris was easy to spot: he was the only guy in the club dressed like me in jeans and a shirt. We stuck out like clowns at a funeral.

'Um, Chris, I'm not sure if you've noticed but tonight is Goth night, mate. Just take a look around you.'

Chris spun round on his chair and surveyed the scene before nodding slowly in agreement and turning back to the barman. 'Two more vodka and Cokes please, mate.'

Regardless of how we were dressed and what type of birthday I was in for, we did manage to attract a few admirers who either took pity on our foolishness or were intrigued by the two 'rebels' of the club.

Whilst I stood among a plethora of gothic smokers neither dressed the same nor with a cigarette in my hand, it was my English accent and pronunciation of the word 'actually' which clearly made one particular girl weak at the knees. During the course of the evening I used the word whenever I possibly could, and after one of the most interestingly strange birthdays of my life wound up paying for a taxi for us to her apartment before returning to my hotel the following morning. With the memories of that night fresh in my mind, I realized that my accent was my secret weapon in the States and it was a trick I was only too happy to have up my sleeve in San Francisco.

Our evening began like any night in Britain for Bateman and me. Eight or ten cans of Budweiser was our standard preliminary to a night on the town. Once these had been taken care of we found ourselves walking back down towards Fisherman's Wharf with me wondering what other words sounded rather spiffing in a well-spoken English accent.

We found a suitable bar near the piers and the evening began like many of my nights back home – a couple more beers for Dutch courage whilst I studied the dance floor for a suitable target. Bateman spotted two unaccompanied young ladies at the bar and so we made our way over to them, positioning ourselves on two of the adjacent seats. The explanation for their unaccompanied status was soon revealed when two blokes sat right next to the girls to continue a conversation they had probably begun seconds before they had left the seats which Bateman and I now occupied. I ordered another drink whilst Bateman went outside for a cigarette.

After ten or fifteen minutes of propping up the bar and drinking by myself, making doubly sure that only the odd one or two people were wearing trench coats, I began to wonder where on earth Bateman had got to. I ventured outside onto the upper decking of the club to investigate. Happily ensconced at the top of the stairway, which many of the club's patrons had turned into a smoking hotspot, were Bateman and two American girls. Just what I needed to get the spree off to a fantastic start in more ways than one. Then, as I approached the girls to introduce myself with the line 'Actually you can call me Rich', or maybe risk a simple but effective 'Actually, actually, actually', I made the shocking discovery that the Americans Bateman had cornered were in fact Swedish. I wasn't sure whether to feel relieved or disheartened. My accent plans would have to change, but, on the other hand, they were Swedish.

'Ah, you must be the law-breaking guy?' remarked Swede One deductively. (I can't remember their names. Shame on me.)

'That's me,' I replied, hoping Bateman hadn't let the cat completely out of the bag. 'So, what brings you to San Francisco?'

42

'Oh, I was an au pair a few years ago and I'm just visiting the family I au-paired for.'

'What's an au pair?' Bateman quickly interjected.

'Remember that Louise girl who was accused of killing that American baby by shaking it a few years back?' I said brightly. Bateman nodded. 'That's what they do.'

Bateman laughed. The Swedes didn't.

'I'm sure you didn't do that, though,' I added quickly. Good start, Rich. Maybe 'Actually, actually, actually' wasn't that foolish an introduction after all.

Back inside, we scuttled them onto the dance floor and instantly gained their admiration when Bateman demanded the DJ play the song the girls had requested earlier in the evening – 'Dancing Queen' by Abba. I was surprised to find that Swedes One and Two remained with us well after their song had been replaced by all manner of musical styles from hip hop and rap to dance. By now, Swede One was comparing muscles with Bateman, who had stripped down to his vest. The fact that Swede One had sunk to Bateman's level and pulled her shirt up past her shoulder to show off her biceps had me smiling and Swede Two staring at her in disgust. Just when things were looking up, and without one 'actually' leaving my lips, the girls informed us that they had a plane to catch in the morning and went off with a brief parting kiss. Minutes later the house lights lit up the dance floor, the music ceased, and there was no time left to find the kind of desperate American girl I should have targeted at the very beginning of the night. I had failed. I had only given myself twenty-four hours in which to break a law in San Francisco, and now my chance had gone. Bateman was definitely not an option.

Next morning the bitter feeling of defeat was out-muscled by the hangover that was pounding through my head. I wasn't too disheartened, considering the nature of the law, but I was eager to get at least one crime under my belt. To achieve that I would have to get out of San Francisco. I was already tired of the constant drone of traffic outside my hotel room, but the only chance we had of leaving was to add to it. Without a car we were stranded in the city and the whole crime spree would centre on my sordid attempts to break the same law over and over again.

Budget was the closest, indeed only, car rental company within easy walking distance; and having learned the hard way that ascending Everest-like hills in San Francisco pulling suitcases was a bad idea, we visited the Budget office and were greeted by an elderly gentleman called Si. He offered us a car for eight hundred dollars, which seemed like a fair price. I already had visions of me at the helm of a blue convertible cruising down the West Coast with the refreshing northerly wind in my hair, two gorgeous female hitch-hikers in the back seat and Bateman in the boot.

That was until Si realized that neither of us was twenty-five. This proved to be a big insurance problem, the effect of which was to raise the overall price by about a million per cent. We left downhearted and empty-handed.

After several more failed attempts to hire a car ourselves using the pay phone outside our motel and a page we had unceremoniously torn out of the Yellow Pages, I did what any hardened law-breaking criminal would do in this situation – I rang my mother.

She secured us a vehicle using the Internet at home, thus becoming a fully fledged aider and abetter. In no time at all, Bateman and I found ourselves back at the airport to pick up a car. It was a 2005 Chrysler Sebring and would be ours for the next three weeks, until we reached Chicago where, due to the mother-rental agreement, a new car would have to be hired for the jaunt to New York. The Sebring was brand new and had no miles on the clock. We would soon fix that. We headed south on Route 1 towards Los Angeles. We were on the road (albeit on the wrong side) and heading into the unknown in what I suppose would become our version of a getaway car.

Twenty minutes out of San Francisco the cool bay-side temperatures had given way to the exhausting heat of inland California. The air-conditioning soon became a necessity, and all in all driving in America was far from cool. Much of this could be attributed to the automatic transmission. Simply put, it removes all the pleasure, instinct and skill from driving. Back in the UK, I'd have changed gears weeks ago, but here we were at the mercy of the engine's whims, regardless of our pleas, cries, demands and eventual yells of frustration at the dashboard. Cruise control was handy, but when added to the already deadening sensation of driving without a gear stick generated an experience behind the wheel which verged on the mind-numbingly mundane. Boredom was eventually beaten when we began a US version of our favourite motorway travel game – Spot the Roadkill.

We headed back towards the coast in search of the Pacific Coast Highway, turning off the interstate and consulting a map to discover the best way of cutting through the Santa Lucia mountain range which separated us from the sea. We didn't choose very wisely. Every 'town' the road passed through seemed to be populated solely by farm animals, and the mountains, which by now had surrounded us, were bare, desolate rock faces where not even beasts dared to tread. Eventually, after a few wrong turns, we met another human being who was happy to direct us to the coast. Unfortunately, he was a member of the US army and his recommended route passed through the Fort Hunter Liggett Military Reservation, which we were free to travel on once he had seen my licence and rental agreement. Our every action was probably being monitored back in the barracks as we passed a forecourt where no fewer than twenty tanks and other military vehicles stood. One false move and we could be subjected to America's trademark 'friendly fire'. The road meandered along before finally climbing through the mountains to the coast. At the top of the mountain – surprisingly temperatures there reached 38 degrees – the Pacific was directly in front of us. Pity the fog meant that only a cloud-filled valley was visible. To make matters worse, Bateman led the road-kill game a rabbit to nil.

After four hours on the road, and exactly halfway down the coast from San Francisco to Los Angeles, we arrived at a tidy Morro Bay motel as the evening grew darker and the sun descended into the Pacific to the west. After the hectic first few days of flights, car worries and law-breaking failure, it was good to feel relaxed and at total ease with the surroundings. Palm trees stood just feet from our door, the Pacific rolled gallantly onto the shores just beyond, and a man nearby was shouting profanities and vicious threats at the owners of the house opposite our motel.

From what I could make out from the bathroom, where his voice could be heard the clearest, he was obviously drunk but still had some harsh words to say to Chico and two others whose names I couldn't make out through his drunken ramblings. Stepping out onto the balcony with a slice of pizza in hand to see if I could see what was going on, I heard that he wanted to slice their necks and quickly returned to the bathroom where I was safe from becoming his next victim. After thirty of the most entertaining minutes I have ever spent in a bathroom, listening to more blasphemies, curses and expletives than I thought existed, the police arrived and took the man away.

*

Baldwin Park, a suburb-cum-city of Los Angeles, was my next target. In Baldwin Park it is illegal to ride a bike in a swimming pool, which seemed like a very rock 'n' roll law to break. After leaving Morro Bay we detoured slightly to visit Hearst Castle, which stands on the hills overlooking San Simeon and the Pacific. US publisher William Randolph Hearst's immaculate 'ranch' wasn't constructed until the media mogul was in his forties as his parents forbade it, saying he would 'go too far'. In 1919, only two months after his mother died and he inherited her vast wealth, Hearst, on whom the famous film *Citizen Kane* is based, and architect Julia Morgan stood on the empty hills and began to make his parents' premonition come true by starting construction on a home comprising fifty-six bathrooms, sixty-one bedrooms and its own cinema. As Bateman and I stepped onto the bus that winds the seven miles up the mountains from the coast, I naturally jumped onto the five seats which make up the back seat as if this was a school trip, and the educational impression was reinforced by the pre-recorded talk on the history of the castle which was timed perfectly to match the duration of the drive. The tour company caters for Europeans rather too well and every time a unit of weight, size, distance or height was mentioned a conversion was guaranteed to follow. The constant changing of pounds to kilos, miles to kilometres and feet to metres made the tape last twice as long as necessary, and when we finally reached the gates of the castle I felt as if I should never require the use of a conversion table again.

Bill, our guide, welcomed us as we stepped off the bus and then marched up to the top of the castle's granite steps and talked us through the rules of the visit – 'keep within the velvet ropes', 'don't lose the rest of the group', et cetera.

'And, kids, if you're thinking of throwing a coin into the fountain and making a wish, I guarantee you, there's more chance of that wish coming true if you keep hold of your money.'

As Bill cracked the same jokes he has probably trotted out for the twenty-six years that he has been a Hearst Castle guide, I began to feel less like an aspiring criminal and more like a camera-wielding tourist. This was probably due to the fact that I was in a foreign country and carrying a camera. I wanted to feel infamous, not one of the crowd, and as I am one of those people who tend not to brag about the English heritage and probably take it for granted, it was really grating on my nerves that the remainder of the group seemed to praise everything they saw. The constant and completely unnecessary wows, gee whizzes and once 'You'd better believe it' voiced by the American contingent of our group made me long only to return to the bus and remind myself again how many acres make up a hectare. One lady asked if the living room furniture had been here when Hearst was in residence after Bill had already explained twice that nothing had been altered; a girl was told off numerous times for touching the marble and leaning on several household items; and I can't remember the number of times a camera flash went off although we'd been told it was strictly forbidden. Not that I really cared, but it was making Bill pretty twitchy. Just when I thought that the tour couldn't end quickly enough, we entered the final and my favourite room.

Hearst's Roman pool, styled in imitation of the baths of Caracalla in ancient Rome, typifies the whole palatial complex. The walls, covered in mosaic tile patterns inspired by Italian mausoleums, together with the eight marble statues of Greek and Roman gods which surround the pool, exude a profound air of significant affluence and astronomic extravagance, and the roof, adorned with stars and other galactic entities, produces a truly out-of-this-world experience. We were told that the tiles which line the pool and cover the walls from ceiling to floor are an inch square, were all fitted individually and occupied half of the builders' seven-year construction time to place. Even I, refined and English as I was, had to contain an unnecessary whooping noise after that statistic.

The timing of our arrival in Los Angeles wasn't great. Traffic in LA is pretty much constant but rush hour is at its peak at five – when we arrived. The city produces the kind of traffic jam where reaching speeds in excess of 20 mph feels as if you have broken the sound barrier. Not even the twelve-lane highways that cater for LA's thousands of commuters are large enough to cope with the traffic's demands. Progress was slow and it took us two or three hours to travel just twenty-five miles east of the city to Baldwin Park.

Law number two was actually quite a challenge. I needed to enlist a motel proprietor who would understand what I was trying to do, and allow me to do it. Or not actively prevent me, if he was anxious about aiding and abetting a career criminal. I was confident that hiring a bike would not be a problem.

Bitter disappointment: who would have foreseen that the suburb would have only a public swimming pool? Baldwin Park was a Mexican neighbourhood, and out of the three shabby motels we found there, not a single one of them had a pool. Using the public swimming pool would have qualified, I felt, but would be too much hassle, and it would be very difficult to smuggle a push bike through the showers towards the poolside. The motel where we eventually stayed was only a mile away in the neighbouring suburb of El Monte. The accommodation was far better than what we had seen in Baldwin Park and we had full use of all the motel's amenities: cable TV, fridge, iron and ironing board and, ironically, a swimming pool.

I had only been in America for four days and already I had been defeated by the two laws I had attempted to break. Admittedly, they were difficult laws to contravene, but in my mind the bottom line was that I had failed and that I didn't like. Suddenly inspiration struck, and I instantly ran to the shop opposite the motel to check out the fruit and veg section.

Californian law states that you are prohibited from peeling oranges in a hotel room. My frustration had reached boiling point and I simply had to break the run of bad luck we were having, even if my crime wasn't as dramatic as riding a bike in a pool or receiving oral sex. I wound up spitting in the face of authority by peeling not one orange but three.

That'll show 'em.

4

Californian Crime Wave

There was still one law that I wanted to tackle in Los Angeles before we moved on. Cursing on a mini-golf course in Long Beach sounded easy to break and would be attempted later on in the afternoon when the fiery temperature fell back into the twenties. I'd heard a lot about American miniature golf courses and from what I'd seen in films and on TV they are anything but miniature. I was expecting giant clown heads and twenty-foot windmills where a good stroke would involve placing the ball between the blades as they rotated and landing it safely on the green. To be honest, anything would have been an improvement on the British version of the game where the toughest shot choice you'll encounter is deciding at which side of the building brick to aim.

I hated Los Angeles. It was a seemingly endless urban sprawl that stretched inland for forty miles from the Pacific, the city and its suburbs continuing well into the desert. Bateman and I decided to visit some of LA's famous surfing spots – hoping that this might give us a better impression of the place – before making our way back up the coast to Long Beach and one of its mini-golf courses.

Since surfing first hit the mainstream with help from films like *Endless Summer* (1966), Huntington Beach with its prominent and unmistakable pier has become a Californian Mecca for surfers and the day of our visit was no exception. Even though it was just an ordinary Wednesday morning when you'd think people should be either at work or doing chores, the sea was peppered with body boarders, surfers and the ubiquitous and obligatory long boarders (the perennial exponents of 'old school' and 'natural' surfing). Behind us, yet more hopefuls were crossing the road with their boards under their arms, hurriedly passing people who had donned their sandals and slung towels over their shoulders to simply enjoy the beach. We realized that the American summer holidays had begun two weeks before and this accounted for the weekday crowds. From the pier, children could be seen playing volleyball on one of the many courts which paralleled the beachside footpath, or simply enjoying the beach and the thought of their twelve weeks in the sun. Lucky sods.

Although Huntington was technically a suburb of

Los Angeles, we were far enough away from the noise, crowds and crisscross of a multitude of inter-states to actually get out of our car and enjoy the town, its pier and its people, whose only rush seemed to be in the direction of the water.

After a brief pit-stop in Huntington, Newport was next on the list, only about twenty miles further down the coast. I needed to find an Internet café to email the children at the primary school where I used to work, as I had promised to keep the class up to date on my adventures and to respond if they emailed me. Newport Beach had evolved from a simple surfing hotspot to a prosperous city with a population of over 70,000, so I thought I'd have no problem whatsoever finding somewhere to email from. We followed the signs that directed us to tourist information. From there we were directed to the nearby mall where we were told to go to the library. I couldn't believe I hadn't thought of the library before. A free Internet café which provided every service a café did bar the muffins.

I quickly typed the email to Mr Rice's class, attached a few pictures and openly invited questions from the children. Not wishing to corrupt young minds, I mentioned nothing of the true reason for my visit to the US and most of the email was about my visit to Hearst Castle and the weather – well, you have to, don't you? Leaving the library, Bateman and I visited the Newport Wedge, a famous 'shore dump' where the waves (that break directly onto the sand) can reach heights in excess of twenty feet. Today the sea was like a millpond and a couple who passed me on a tandem seemed more threatening. It was time to leave. The hour for cussing, blasphemy and unnecessary but intentional four-letter faux pas on the miniature golf course was almost upon us.

The drive to Long Beach would take us back through Huntington along the coastal road. Bateman was driving – theoretically so that I could make notes on our travels to date but also so that I could sightsee. Petrol stations and fast-food chains I expected to pass regularly, but for every mile we drove more and more palm readers and psychics were plying their trade and using bigger and better signs to attract potential customers. Back home I wouldn't know where to go to visit a psychic and now I was being offered palm readings and visions of my future at almost every set of traffic lights. After passing the fifth one in five minutes, psychic pressure was getting to me. I decided that owing to the uncertainty of my future in the States I ought to pay one a visit and would do so when we eventually reached Long Beach. Before that happened, however, we had met our first American roundabout. I know that I shouldn't find a round-about as impressive as I did that day, but, after not having taken a single photograph when I was in San Francisco, I quickly produced my camera to capture our first encounter with a 'traffic circle'.

Now I know what you're thinking: what's so special

about a roundabout? If you're English, nothing much; if you're an Englishman in America, a great deal. I once travelled around America with my dad and in five weeks drove more than eleven thousand miles. In all that time, we came across one single roundabout (incidentally, it was the Long Beach one and we were so shocked by its sudden approach that we took the wrong turning). One appearance in eleven thousand miles makes whichever roundabout you do see something very special indeed. In the UK you can barely drive on a main road for more than eleven miles without encountering a traffic system which keeps cars moving instead of the four-way traffic lights that are so popular in the States.

Just up the road from the splendour of the roundabout I spotted a psychic whose sign wasn't easily missed. I was expecting a Madame Enigma or something similar, but the thirty-foot billboard which stood in her front garden informed me that my future would be seen by Brenda – a rather bland name for a psychic. Brenda operated her business from her home in a rather prosperous area of Long Beach, and apart from the massive sign the house seemed pretty normal, with a cupboard for sale for forty dollars on the front lawn. Tentatively I climbed the steps to the front door and tapped nervously on the insect-proof screen door frame.

The door opened and revealed a woman in her early fifties with tied-back ginger hair. She clutched the door knob in one hand and a bowl of stir-fry in the other and stared vacantly at me as if I were a door-to-door salesman.

'Hi. Are you ... um ... open?' I asked, not really sure of what the term for a currently operating psychic would be.

'Yes, I am. Come in,' she replied, her mood changing completely. Now she was upbeat and ready to go, like a school kid who had been kept in class for ten extra minutes and had finally been released into the playground and wanted to make up for lost time.

Bateman and I sat in her porch, which seemed to also function as her consulting room. The porch was cosy and looked as if it were split into halves. The left-hand side, where Bateman perched, was dotted with Buddhist statues and randomly placed Irish memorabilia from Guinness posters to shamrock and leprechauns. I sat in the right-hand half, which was dominated by dozens of porcelain statues, shelves of postcards and framed pictures of the Messiah; and a single style-his-hair troll (remember those from the nineties?) and the compulsory crystal ball were the only non-Christian items in sight.

As I began to do an impersonation of Mystic Meg, I was disturbed by Brenda who emerged from the house and positioned herself opposite me. Sitting this close to her, I could clearly see two boils which instead of being on her nose, as you'd expect, were situated between her neck and her chest.

'What do you want? Tarot cards, palm reading or your future read?' she asked.

'I'll have the cheapest, please.' And anything that didn't involve looking into her crystal boils.

'If you want to know how your trip in the States will go, it'll be the future reading,' she replied. Obviously that was the most expensive.

'To read your fortune, I will need something that is yours and has only belonged to you,' she instructed. The only things I had on me were my clothes, which I was planning on keeping on, and coins which I was sure someone had previously owned.

'How about a flip-flop?' I asked, thinking on (and about) my feet, and proffered one in her direction.

'No, that won't do!' she said sternly.

'I haven't stepped in anything,' I said in an attempt to break the ice the shoe-offering had created. What was wrong with a flip-flop anyway? I had had sole ownership of it and, to be honest, was finding it hard to take this whole process seriously.

'How about your sunglasses?' she asked, pointing at my neck, round which they hung.

Like a pencil behind the ear, I had completely forgotten they were there. I gave them to Brenda. She held them in both hands and pulled them close to her chest – too close to the boils for my liking.

'Yes, you are a strong man. You like to be independent and you were born to be successful.'

'OK,' I replied, knowing full well that it was probably the usual spiel she used to put her client at ease.

'By the end of the year I can see a change of location for you.'

'I was planning on moving house by the end of the year actually,' I said. My scepticism was still strong, but by now Brenda was in full swing.

'You will be happy with a girl but there will come a time when you must decide between two.'

'Two? That many?' I replied with a smile. Just as I was beginning to enjoy myself, Brenda's permanent smile turned upside down.

'Don't get into a red car,' she warned, making serious eye contact.

'Pardon?'

'Someone will offer you a lift in a red car during your stay here. Don't get in. Danger,' she reiterated.

'Thank God our hire car is blue,' I joked, but Brenda was far from laughing.

'Beware of a white-, silver- or blond-haired man. He cannot be trusted financially.'

'O . . . K, although that does only leave me with black or ginger-haired people. Anything else?' I enquired. There was silence.

'I see, I see . . . a court case.'

'Great. Just what I need.'

'Someone will take what you're doing seriously and you will appear in court.'

I had told her why I was in America and so wasn't particularly impressed. 'Can I have some nice stuff again?' I asked.

'You will invent something and make money out of it.' I wasn't sure what that would be and stared blankly back at Brenda with my bottom lip protruding to show the fact. 'Do you know what it is?'

'Nope,' I replied.

'Are you sure?'

Even if I did know I wasn't going to tell her. I wasn't going to let her steal my idea. 'No, I seriously don't know.' Maybe my sunglasses told Brenda something or I had foiled her hope of blatant plagiarism, because she instantly changed the subject for the worse.

'In the next eight weeks, someone will confront you and you must walk away.'

I stared at Bateman and pointed at him.

'Oh, no. I'm sure it won't be your friend.'

'It probably will be, you know,' he said, sitting back in his chair, as if he had already had that premonition himself.

'Yeah, and I'm a coward and always walk away anyway. I even run sometimes,' I added.

After several startling revelations about my owning my own business, Brenda asked me if I had any questions about my future.

'Only one,' I replied. 'Is there a mini-golf course in Long Beach?'

'No,' she replied.

'Shit. Are you sure?' My scepticism regarding psychics had reached an all-time high.

'I'm positive. My husband and I used to play a lot of mini-golf and the course in Long Beach closed two years after we were married in . . . what must it have been now? . . . 1971.'

'So I'm a tad late then? Are you absolutely positive

that there isn't one within the Long Beach city limits? Not even by the *Queen Mary*? Loads of tourists go there.'

'You can use the Net and look if you want.'

I was invited inside and found that the closest miniature golf course to Long Beach was in a town called Wilmington, two miles away.

As I left her house, I turned to Brenda and put a question I had wanted to ask when she first opened the door. Then I had felt it would be rude and unnecessary to put such a question to a woman who was, after all, my hostess. Now, though, she was the woman who had broken devastating news to me about the mini-golf course. In my mind she was responsible for the third failure of the holiday so far and deserved everything she got.

'If you're such a good psychic, why don't you just display the cupboard on the lawn on days you know someone who will buy it is going to walk by?' That told her.

I hated Los Angeles. Hated it. I needed some cheering up, and Bateman was certainly not equipped for the job.

'So much for the spree, Rich,' he said. 'You may as well just write a detailed account of the roadkill we find. At least we've had a lot of success there.'

'Hey, things'll pick up,' I replied, trying to convince myself. 'It's just not the best of starts. That's all'

Before we could leave the city, Bateman, a habitual gym user back home, insisted we visit Venice Beach and the famous Muscle Beach gym, once the cradle of gymnastic exhibitions but now frequented mainly by bodybuilders. Most important, he wanted to buy an Arnold Schwarzenegger 'Governator' T-shirt. After visiting the gym, where Bateman finally selected a 'My Governor Can Kick Your Governor's Ass' T-shirt, we decided to get a bite to eat before leaving town.

Only two blocks from Santa Monica pier is a branch of the restaurant chain called Hooters. The bright white and orange colour scheme made us think of the old diner days of America in the fifties, but as we stepped inside what was on show was anything but a reminder of more conservative times.

Bateman and I were shown to our seat by Jen, a stunningly attractive girl who, like all the other waitresses, was dressed in nothing more than a white vest and very tiny orange skin-hugging shorts. I went for the Hooters Burger which when ordered sounded like some sort of obscure German musical instrument. Just as our food arrived, 'YMCA' by the Village People came blasting out of the speaker system and floor service went on hold as all the waitresses climbed on any furniture that happened to be in their vicinity to dance. The table next to ours comprised two teenagers and their grandmother, and when the dancing began I looked across to see the reaction of a shocked pensioner who had just realized the true reason why her grandchildren insisted on eating here. To my surprise, the boys were trying to pretend they found the bubbles in their fizzy drinks more entertaining than the free show, whilst their grandmother was applauding and cheering every shoulder-shake and bottom-wiggle.

If the dancing, the cheap pitchers of beer and the nine raised television screens, all showing sport from baseball to women's volleyball, didn't sum up the place, the sign I noticed above the door as we left certainly did. 'Men: No Shirt, No Service. Women: No Shirt, Free Food.'

It was time for Bateman and me to join an endless queue of traffic and take the crammed six-lane highway eastward out of the city.

At 6 p.m., after almost three hours, the Los Angeles gridlock finally subsided and gave way to open lanes. We were now more than thirty miles outside downtown and drawing near to Palm Springs, a city that stands alone amidst towering desert mountains. The evening temperature was still unbearably hot and we took a dip in the motel's swimming pool, which did nothing to cool us down. The heat of the day, which had remained at a constant 43 degrees, had easily warmed the small pool up and our 'cool-down' swim was taken in water which was hotter than I usually have in my bath.

Next morning we paid a visit to the nearby library in Cathedral City to check our emails. The Riverside County Library Service was now the third of which I was a member. Is this the mark of a wise man or a cheapskate? As expected, the email reply from the children lay in my inbox and I opened up, unsure what kind of questions they were going to ask. As far as I knew, only one of the children, an impish boy called Joel, knew why I was really here, as I had met him at a cricket match shortly before I had left and had told him everything. The rest of his class thought I was simply in America for a holiday.

Joel must have said something.

'How are you going to get a giraffe?' wrote Kane and Damon, before asking, 'Do you know where the cheese factory you're going to fall asleep in is?'

Christopher, who didn't know it at the time, added salt to my healing wounds by asking: 'Have you found a bike and a swimming pool yet?'

The questions that followed were simpler and closer to what I was expecting. Chantelle, Emily and Hayley enquired as to how cold it was at the top of the mountain where I had taken the pictures and the rest of the girls affectionately stated that they missed me and wanted me to come back – before bizarrely asking if I'd seen a baby koala. Meanwhile, Joel, who had begun the interrogation, along with Luke and Samuel, had addressed more pressing, grown-up matters and asked: 'How are the chicks?' But it was Ben and Jake who asked the most important question of the lot: 'When are you going to stop being silly?' I've yet to get back to them on that one.

Indian Wells citation 9.04.020 (Musical Instruments – Use in attracting customers for sales) decrees that: 'It is declared to be a nuisance and it is unlawful for any person vending, advertising or soliciting the sale of, or assisting in vending, advertising or soliciting the sale of any kind of notions, merchandise or medicines in the City to use a musical instrument or device, or to sing or call out or to make any noise to attract persons for the purpose of vending, advertising or soliciting the sale of notions, medicines or merchandise.'

O . . . K.

So in order to get this crime spree back on track, in layman's terms I had to play a musical instrument with the intention of luring someone into a shop. Easy. I headed to Toys 'Я' Us for the tools I'd require. Never having played a trumpet before, I was not at all sure what I should buy, but luckily only one model was on offer.

For a mere $8.99 I purchased what I can only describe as a three-in-one electronic trombone, trumpet and saxophone (because that was what was written on the packaging). After taking the batteries out of my digital camera and putting them in the instrument, it was time to find an ideal place to put my snake charmer-like tones into practice. A nearby arcade of stores seemed like a nice spot in which to play and a position outside an antique shop was selected. Several people passed and stared at me strangely but not a single one decided to enter the shop. But they didn't need to. The law stated I had to have the intention, not that I had to actually lure them in, and as I began to direct their attention by raising my eyebrows and tilting my head towards the shop door it was clear what my overall aim was. After several minutes, with no customers and slightly sore fingers, I removed the trumpet from my lips, took a bow, and pressed one of the sound effect buttons on the side of the toy to produce a rapturous applause, congratulating myself on a law well broken. It was just a pity there was no one there to see it.

5

Showdown at the Saloon

The 'Welcome To Arizona – The Grand Canyon State' sign was truly a welcome sight for me. My expectations after putting the disappointment of California behind me were as high as the temperature, which by now had reached a stupidly high 49 degrees. The searing desert heat meant leaving the car was to be attempted only if absolutely necessary and the air conditioner was having to work overtime. Back home, people complain when temperatures spill into the thirties, so this sort of level was uncomfortable for locals, let alone people who aren't used to the heat.

Unlike California, Arizona had only one law for me to break and our destination was the small town of Globe, 230 miles east of the border, where it's illegal to play cards against a Native American. The earlier illegal activity in Indian Wells had resulted in a later than normal start and it was decided we would spend a night in Phoenix.

We checked into a hotel to the south of the city and as I sat in the lobby to make use of their free Internet access, it wasn't long before Jennifer, the desk clerk, began talking to me, seemingly about anything that came into her head.

'So you guys spell tyre with a Y, huh? How strange.'

The constant interruptions meant that one email took more than an hour to write, but by the time I finished I had managed to consume four cans of lager, taught Jennifer about the British Empire and come to sympathize with the Tower of London guards who had got annoyed with Jennifer and her friends on her recent visit to the English capital.

Bateman returned from using the hotel's gym and joined me in the lobby with his own can of lager. For a Friday night, the hotel was very quiet and drinking seemed the only activity worth pursuing. It wasn't long before we were joined by Joye, a delightfully amiable woman who lived in Flagstaff and was visiting her Honduran-born mother who worked in the hotel. During the ensuing conversation I discovered that Joye used to live in Globe and asked her what I should expect from the town and, more important, how difficult a Native American would be to find.

'You shouldn't have too much of a problem finding an Indian in Globe,' Joye explained encouragingly, while simultaneously scoffing at my interest in the town. 'Any bar'll have quite a few, I reckon.'

After several declined offers, Joye finally accepted one of our cans, endearingly referring to it as a 'pint'. 'I'll only have one,' she explained, 'I have to be up early tomorrow.'

It didn't take long, probably owing to Jennifer's perpetual presence behind the desk, before the conversation turned to America's education system, about which I have only ever heard bad things. I had expected Joye and Jennifer to defend their country but Joye was definitely not sluggish in her response. 'It's terrible. Especially here in Arizona.'

'I've heard that some high school graduates can't even point to America on an unmarked globe and assume Russia is it because it's the biggest. Is that true?' I asked.

'I wouldn't be surprised. They aren't the brightest,' Joye replied. Jennifer didn't agree with us but was caught short when asked where Beijing was. She was surprised by the answer. 'Is it? Well, I thought it wasn't in America.'

Next morning I awoke fully clothed and realized I was up early enough to make use of the hotel's breakfast service. The dining room was practically empty and I sat down next to the only occupied table, beside a couple who appeared to be the only other guests in the hotel: Joye and her mother.

'Mom, this is Richard. He's one of the cleverest guys I've met. He's the one going around America to break all the silly laws,' said Joye as I struggled to open a

cereal packet, thereby proving Joye's kind introduction to be a very inaccurate one.

'Hi. Very pleased to meet you. Joye tells me you're
originally from Honduras,' I replied, ripping the
packet of Lucky Charms open as I spoke and scatter-
ing cereal everywhere.

Since an early age, I've always retained strange facts
about countries and have often taken pride in recall-
ing them, although so far they have proved to be
nothing more than useless information that has
stubbornly resisted any attempt to remove it from my
brain. By now I must possess a fact for most countries
in the Western world and I suppose I always hope
these will stand me in good stead if ever I want to
sound intelligent in the presence of a foreign national.
For some reason I am aware that Canada has more
land water than the rest of the world put together, I
know Tajikistan is the home of the world's tallest dam
and I can hum the Qatari national anthem.
Honduras's fact was easy to recall owing to the fact
that it was a 'double-whammy' and could be used for
two countries.

'Were you there when Honduras had a six-day
war with El Salvador over a World Cup qualifying
match?' I asked excitedly (it was one of my favourite
facts).

'Oh. Yes. It was terrible; there was panic in the
streets. Riots and rapes were frequent and my parents
hated each other. You see, one was Nicaraguan and
the other Honduran.'

Perhaps, in the future, I should stick with the fact that Honduras is the third largest garment supplier to the US.

After saying goodbye to Joye and her mother, it was time to hit the road once more and travel the ninety-two miles east to Globe. Route 60 was a far cry from the interstate roads to which Bateman and I were now accustomed and made its way sinuously through rugged, cacti-ridden landscapes which painted a harsh picture of bleak and inhospitable surroundings. The towns we passed were unremarkable and easily forgettable and it seemed no time at all before the road made its final turn through the Superstition Mountains and we saw the town of Globe ahead of us.

You'd be easily forgiven for thinking Globe's population was much greater than the official figure of a little over 7,000, if you saw the number of motels that greeted our arrival, and it seems that every fast food brand in the country is represented there. Burger King, McDonald's, Domino's Pizza and Taco Bell all vie for customers on a stretch of road where a stables and blacksmith's shop would seem more appropriate.

We decided to combat the heat with a quick swim in our motel's swimming pool, which was conveniently located just outside our door. After a quick dip among the uninvited leaves and crisp packets, we had returned to our room to discuss tactics when the weather took a decided turn for the worse.

The small white clouds which had hung in the sky as we drove into town had vanished, replaced by what was now a menacing grey sheet. As I began to dry myself off, the sky became darker and released a cacophonic crash of thunder which resonated through the town as the heavens opened. In a matter of seconds, the rain had turned the flower bed outside our door into a pool of murky water and the winds had picked up to a terrifying speed. I slammed the door firmly shut and for a moment we watched the mayhem from the comfort of our room. Then Bateman had a brainstorm.

'Back in the pool!' he shouted at the top of his lungs.

'What?' Sometimes I marvel at his stupidity.

'In the spa. It'll be warm in there. It'll be great,' he replied with a certain degree of persuasive logic. Well, enough to send us out into the storm and into the spa.

As we lay in the jet-streamed warm waters of the spa, the storm howled and wailed with increasing ferocity and the raindrops which pounded into my cheeks and eyes felt as hard as hail. The buildings on the other side of the road had by now become invisible behind a curtain of rain and the crisp packets with which we had previously shared the pool had been swept away. As the winds increased, Bateman and I were reduced to shouting at each other in any attempts to communicate, and amid the crashes of thunder and fork lightning which illuminated the dull and dismal sky I wondered if it wouldn't now be a better plan to go back indoors. The decision was finally cemented when a poolside umbrella, which had been spectacularly blown over earlier, suddenly caught the wind and rushed towards me with terrifying speed. At the last moment, it wedged itself into the steps used to enter the pool – directly in front of where I was sitting.

We raced back to our room and as quickly as it had arrived the storm lost strength, the clouds parted allowing the sun to once again beat down upon the town, and Globe was exactly as it had been when we had arrived an hour before, albeit a bit more soggy.

By now it was early evening, and although the temperature was still in the high thirties it was time to leave the motel and make our way to the historic downtown area where bars, shops and hopefully Native Americans could be found. As we left, we waved to the motel manager, who was still trying to fish the remaining pool furniture out of the deep end.

Downtown Globe was a ghost town. There were people about, quite a few, but it's how I have always pictured an old cowboy town to be: a single, dusty road with buildings hugging the streets and more or less nothing of any interest at either end. As Bateman and I strolled up the main street, it seemed as if it could still be used as a setting for a John Wayne or Clint Eastwood movie. Not even the neon 'open' signs which are ever-present in small-town America and the rows of diagonally parked pick-up trucks were enough to break my reverie of times of lawlessness and showdowns at high noon. At the side of the road, a plaque dedicated to the law enforcement of Gila

County commemorated the 'Hanging Tree' where L. V. Grime and C. B. Hawley were lynched for the hold-up and murder of three men on 24 August 1882. A shop awning had been brought down during the storm and the proprietors were examining the damage; across the road the local cinema had been gutted by a recent fire, and the town's historic air was getting the better of me. The damage to the shop was caused this afternoon and the fire had swept through the building just a week ago, but my overactive imagination decided that the awning had fallen in a shootout and the culprits had eventually been flushed out of their cinema hideout when the sheriff ordered his men to blitz the building.

Back to the task in hand. We needed to find a Native American and acting on Joye's earlier advice Bateman and I peered through restaurant and bar windows in order to find one. Early inspections weren't successful but we put this down to the fact that it was still only five o'clock on a Saturday evening. The most promising bar in town seemed to be the Drift Inn Saloon, which had tables outside, and since the finer points of the law decreed that cards were not to be played on the street with a Native American it seemed the obvious choice of watering hole. The building's likeness to Wild West drinking establishments made entering it seem a daunting prospect, and as soon as we did so all my earlier cowboy dreams came flooding back.

The saloon was founded in 1902 and judging by the lack of air-conditioning and the layout of the bar it seemed that only the clientele and the brands of drinks had changed much since then. Tables stood empty and the fifteen or so stools at the bar provided adequately for the evening patrons. Men in white vests and baseball caps sat alongside butch women with tattoos, a Hispanic lady was serving behind the bar and two young men traded shots on the pool table. Not one of them looked Native American. We took two empty seats at the bar and ordered a couple of bottles of Bud. I was quietly hoping that an Indian would simply walk into the room, but after the disappointing start in California I was determined to see this one through, no matter how long it took. After fifteen minutes of waiting, Bateman and I moved over to the pool table to pass more time and from there I had a superb vantage point for the rest of the bar. After a couple of games, I became aware that two people were paying close attention to us. One was a pug-nosed man who was sitting at the end of the bar and watched our games intently, as if he had a wager on the outcome, and the other was a younger guy dressed in T-shirt and ripped jeans who was using the table next to ours.

'Who just won that game?' asked the young man as he approached to shake our hands.

'Um . . . he did,' replied Bateman, pointing his cue at me.

'You want a match?'

When I broke, the young man chalked his cue and took his opening shot. 'We'll play your pool rules, shall we? English rules.'

'In that case, that was a foul,' I replied. 'You didn't even hit a ball.'

As the game progressed, I noticed that either he was purposely playing badly in a very poor hustling attempt or he was simply drunk. I won the game quite easily and waited to refuse his request for a rematch – this time for money. It never came.

'So what you doing in Arizona?' he asked as we both placed our cues back in the rack to confirm that there was to be no rematch.

'I'm here looking for a Native American really. You don't happen to know any, do you?' I asked hopefully.

He looked right into my eyes and approached me. 'You can't turn back the hands of time, man.'

'Right,' I said, not knowing what on earth that was supposed to mean. He staggered back to his friend. I took that as a no, then.

We returned to the bar. By now an hour had elapsed, with no Native American encounters and just a pool victory over a drunkard under my belt. As we ordered our next drink, I asked the bartender if Indians often drank here. Her answer appeared to be a wild guess but was more than encouraging. 'Yeah. We're expecting one any minute now.'

'Any minute now' turned to ten minutes now and ten to twenty. I was beginning to grow impatient as the temperature began to drop and, with it, the sun's position in the sky. Just as I was beginning to think about changing bars and maybe having to resign myself to another night in Globe, a man walked up the steps and entered the room. I only got a quick glimpse of him as he strode past me before perching himself on an empty seat at the opposite end of the bar, but his jet-black moustache and rough, tanned skin made me feel that my wait might be at an end. I quickly stood up and examined him further. The suspect was dressed casually in jeans, a white T-shirt and the mandatory baseball cap, but I began to picture him in Indian regalia, complete with ceremonial headdress, and felt the bottle of lager in his hand could well have been a tomahawk.

'That's our man!' I said to Bateman. 'Let's go sit by him. There are two empty seats at his side of the bar.'

We positioned ourselves alongside him. Bateman looked on expectantly as I took a few minutes to compose myself and prepare my opening gambit.

What do you say? You don't just ask someone to play cards with you because you think they're an Indian. I thought of offering to buy him a drink but he seemed to have two already and might get the wrong idea about my intentions. Just then, he turned, and the brief pause created my opening.

'Hiya. You couldn't do me a big favour, could you?' I offered my hand for him to shake. 'My name's Richard Smith and I'm over here from England breaking silly laws in America. In Globe it's illegal to play cards against a Native American in the street and I was wondering if you could just have a quick game with me. It'll take just two minutes of your time.'

Remarkably, this didn't faze him at all. The man

took the drink away from his lips, laughed and shook my hand. 'Why sure. It should be fun.'

The Native American's name was Arden Deloris. As we took our seats outside, the light was beginning to fade. A moderate breeze blew down the street, probably a remnant of the earlier storm. I produced a pack of cards from my shorts pocket as Arden opened his wallet in order to show me something.

'This proves how Native American I am,' he said, handing me the driving licence-sized card. It was green, and depicted Arden and the name of his tribe: Laguna Pueblo. 'You see, I speak like a white man, I look like a Mexican but I'm full-blooded Indian,' he added. 'So, what game do you want to play?'

'What games do you know?' I replied.

'Shall we play king's corner?'

'I've never heard of it. Do you know how to play rummy or poker?'

'No.'

So it turned out that finding a Native American was the easy bit. I should have realized, as I've always found it to be the same: between them, any two people know the rules to nearly every card game there is, but very rarely do they share the knowledge of a single one.

'How about snap? I'll teach you the rules to that. It's simple,' I suggested. It took me less than a minute to teach him and a little under a minute later I had one half of the pack, Arden had the other, the game had begun and the law had been broken. Almost instantly two sixes appeared and Arden looked at me as if he wasn't sure what to do.

'Snap!' I said, slamming my hand down on the table and claiming the cards. This blatant act of unsportsmanlike play only injected fire and competition into Arden who won every time from that point on, easily beating me at my own game. I never was good at snap.

'So why is it illegal then?' Arden asked much later than I thought he would.

'I don't know, but in South Dakota three Native Americans walking down the road can be considered a war party and may be fired upon, so you should count yourself lucky that you're only banned from playing cards.' That brought a smile to his face.

Bateman, who had been taking photos of the epic snap battle, had now joined us at the table and we were both engrossed in Arden's tales of his life and his people. For the first time on the trip so far, we sat and listened to a stranger, not interrupting or cracking jokes, but just drinking in every word.

We only did play that one game of snap, but we remained outside well after the sun eventually went down. Over a few drinks, it transpired that Arden will remain in Globe for the next two years as a heavy-machinery worker in the construction industry. The name of his tribe, the Laguna Pueblo, is derived from two sources – the Pueblo are his people and they reside in Laguna, New Mexico. It's an 800-mile round trip from Globe, one that Arden makes every weekend to see his family. He is a proud man who knows his skills are highly regarded by his employer but takes greater pride in his son, an eighteen-year-old who is currently at college in Denver (studying to work in construction like his father). Feeling sentimental, Arden unclipped his mobile phone from his belt to leave a loving message from father to son.

When I asked Arden if he thought working in construction so far away from his tribe meant that he ever felt as if he was losing any of his Native heritage he shook his head.

'I'm one of the few people in my tribe who can still speak the language. I'll teach my son the same way I was taught and I'm hoping he will do the same,' he told me.

By now it was pitch black, and as Arden made his way back inside Bateman and I moved in the opposite direction to the car. Much as I had enjoyed drinking and talking to Arden, tonight had been set aside for a trip to the Indian reservation casino ten miles out of town.

With the law-breaking back on track Bateman and I thought it best if we hired a taxi to take us to and from the casino, so we could both drink and lose money at the same time.

Bateman used the room's phone to call the controller of a nearby taxi company suggested to us by the motel manager. 'Could we get a taxi to the casino at quarter past eight, please? No. A quarter past eight. No. Eight fifteen not eight thirty. A quarter *past* eight.' Whoever was at the other end of the line obviously had a problem with telling the time, and instead of asking the man to arrive at our hotel when the big hand had reached the three Bateman settled for eight o'clock.

Our phone rang at eight on the dot and we made our way to the lobby, where a small man stood clutching a set of keys.

'You wanna go to the casino?'

Now I can't say I was expecting a yellow cab or a stretch limo to be waiting for us, but what I did imagine was at least a taxi sign or plaque of authentication stuck to the rear of the vehicle. This car had neither. The blue 1989 Mercury Grand Marquis, which would never have passed its MOT in England, had no indications or markings to reveal it was a taxi but we were assured it was by the man's wife, who sat at ease in the passenger seat.

'Let's hope it doesn't rain. This baby doesn't do so well in the wet,' she remarked. Bateman and I simply stared at each other across the roof of the car and then entered regardless. I squeezed into the back on the driver's side between workmen's helmets behind me and a selection of coats and other garments on the floor which made it impossible for me to put my feet anywhere but to the side. It was humid and stuffy inside and I would have asked our driver to open his window to aerate the car if the glass had not been replaced by a strip of cardboard fastened to the frame by masking tape. Other than the uncomfortable seating and the worrying condition of the taxi, the ride could not have been more pleasant and I began chatting to the driver. As it turned out, our chauffeur and his wife used to sell medical supplies and now, out of work and with trailer-park rent to pay, had begun renting their car out as a taxi. After trying to explain several times that not all Englishmen live in London and in fact we lived more than 300 miles from the capital, Bateman was handed a flyer by the wife.

'Here's our number when you wanna get picked up later on,' she remarked. 'Don't worry about how late it is.'

The piece of A4 paper she handed to Bateman had 'NEED A RiDE GlobE MiAMi CLAyPooL' crudely written above their telephone number in black biro, and, for some reason, a picture of a tricycle pulling a trailer provided the centrepiece.

'Um . . . thanks,' replied Bateman as he folded up the flyer before placing it in his back pocket.

The car eventually pulled up outside the front doors of the casino and as I tipped the driver handsomely for delivering us safely and not stealing my kidneys, he announced to the door staff in a loud, strong tone: 'Take care of these guys. They're from London!'

After taking two hours to find and play cards against one Native American, we were about to spend the entire evening on a blackjack table in competition with a dozen of them.

6

Call Me Richy

Flagstaff lies a mere ninety miles from the Grand Canyon's southern rim and seemed the perfect place to stay overnight after leaving Globe. Utah, where the next law awaited me, was well within striking distance and as the canyon blocked our path no matter which way we decided to get there, it seemed ridiculous to simply bypass one of the Seven Natural Wonders of the World.

It was nine thirty on a Monday morning when we left our motel and arrived in the centre of town where the laid-back northern Arizona lifestyle had a dramatic effect on rush-hour traffic. As we walked from the library through the main park and into the downtown area, the roads were almost devoid of vehicles and the constant honking of car horns with which we were now familiar was absent. Sidewalks were lined with more trees than people and the panoramic view of the ice-capped mountains which surrounded the town together with the refreshing twenty-degree temperature made the entire experience an extremely pleasant one. We strolled over the train track that bisects Flagstaff just in time to hear the alarm which sounds to welcome the famous Santa Fe Railroad to town. The barriers fell, and the few cars that were left to wait did so patiently while the sixty-five carriages were pulled past at a sauntering pace by six forbidding diesel engines. As the train slowly made its steady ascent into the mountains, I turned to Bateman and remarked on how beautiful the town was and that it was easily my favourite thus far. Bateman's reply was quick and decisively blunt. 'It's rubbish. There's nothing here.' Time for the Canyon, I think.

It's not easy to describe the Grand Canyon. Everyone has seen pictures and knows it's a giant chasm carved into the rocks of the Colorado Plateau like an open wound in the side of the earth. The awe-inspiring view of the prodigious canyon which is now well into its umpteenth millennium of creation shows its true beauty when, with the exception of the click of tourists' cameras, there is silence. In a country where grandeur and magnificence is flaunted and held aloft for all to see, the canyon sits in perfect serenity and peace, safe in the knowledge that its simple existence is its greatest appeal.

We drove to a number of viewing points along the southern rim of the canyon, finishing at Desert View, where the open plains of northern Arizona and southern Utah can be viewed beyond the precipices of the canyon. It was there that I experienced an acute sense of boredom as if I had seen it all before, in that all viewing points, however spectacular, are, in a way, very similar. Admittedly I was ashamed to feel this way and chastened to acknowledge that it is very difficult for me to remain in awe of anything, even on a scale of this magnitude, for a prolonged amount of time. As we were leaving I noticed a word on the map that I had only recently learned. One of the Grand Canyon National Park's points of interest is the ruins of the Tusayan Pueblo, and it seemed a perfect opportunity to gain first-hand experience of my card-playing friend's tribal culture.

The ruins were nothing special and it took less than a quarter of an hour to walk past the two-foot-high remnants of five or so buildings which were first erected over eight hundred years ago. The nearby single-room museum's walls adorned with traditional Puebloan attire, weapons the tribesmen may have used, and artistic perceptions of what the settlement looked like at the height of the tribe's occupation are overshadowed by the view the settlers would have had. Instead of the steep descents of the canyon's ridges and desert plains, the settlement stands in perfect sight of Humphreys Peak, Arizona's highest point, forty-six miles south of the canyon.

As we left the Grand Canyon, passing myriad Indian stalls selling all manner of things tribal, my attention turned to the map to get us off the troublesome mountain roads and back onto the highway where travel was boring but speedy. We crossed the border into Utah and Route 9 seemed the quickest way back to the interstate. It was with some degree of confusion and bewilderment that we found ourselves asked to pay a twenty-dollar entrance fee to Zion National Park. Even though we were only using the road through the park to get back to the interstate, the fee would have to be paid. Bateman wasn't at all pleased.

'Twenty bucks! There was a sign back there that said "Don't feed the animals." I'm gonna run them over, get my money's worth and watch them scrape it up. Bastards.'

I had arranged to stay with my friend Lee James in Salt Lake City because the next law was relevant throughout the entire state of Utah, and by now I thought nothing of driving two hundred miles to see a friend, even if scenery remained mountainous but bland: the lack of roadkill did nothing to ease the boredom, and the appearance of a lighthouse in Cedar City, four hundred miles away from the coast, remained the only thing of any interest during the three-hour drive.

We arrived in Salt Lake City a little after three in the afternoon and parked outside Salt Lake Motorsports where Lee worked. Lee, an eighteen-year-old who'd moved from Cornwall to Salt Lake City with his dad and stepmum almost three years ago, wasn't expecting me so early and as I shook his hand I couldn't contain my shock at how he spoke.

'My God, you even speak like a Yank!' I shouted in the middle of the shop. 'How long did that take to change?'

'Well, I have been here almost three years,' Lee replied, probably thinking he might have made a terrible mistake in inviting me to stay. Lee, who now says 'gas' instead of 'petrol', 'couch' instead of 'settee' but is vehemently proud that he pronounces 'garage' the English way, informed us that he knows of at least two roundabouts near where he lives and would show me when he finished work at six. Until then Bateman and I would have to amuse ourselves. There being no other tourist attraction to speak of, we headed for the Great Salt Lake.

The Saltair, a mosque-style building with dome-capped minarets, is a redundant shadow of its former self. Before the turn of the twentieth century, the building was erected by Mormons to provide a 'wholesome place of recreation', and at its height in the 1920s attracted nearly half a million visitors a year. The once end-of-the-pier attraction now stands in a dilapidated state in front of an empty car park, now more than half a mile away from the water due to years of drought. The inside contains a single shop, leaving the rest of the building empty. The dance floor, once the biggest in the world, leads the way to a grand spiral staircase which arrives at an abandoned mezzanine level of a building which is the third to be built on this site after its predecessors were both lost to fire. Outside, two rusty railway carriages have been left to corrode in the salty environment, the only reminder of times when trains ran throughout the day to cope with the visitors' demands. We walked towards the water's edge across the seemingly solid sand, which when stepped upon cracked like old glass, and were met by a dead fish lying just feet from the shore. Nothing seemed to survive here. The lake, which from the shore appears as wide as any ocean, has a lingering smell of sulphur and, with the exception of hundreds of thousands of flies which cling to the remaining dry sands of the beach, is lifeless and still.

A couple of hours passed quickly and we made our way back to Salt Lake Motorsports, in time to see Lee and a work colleague wheeling the mopeds from outside the front door and into the shop. Lee was accompanied by an attractive girl with long black hair and perfectly straight white teeth whom he introduced as his girlfriend Jen. We followed them in our car to their home in Tooele, a twenty-minute drive away (thirty if you take a detour to show an Englishman an American roundabout).

'I got a caution from the police because I left skid marks on top of this roundabout,' he said proudly. 'You want me to show you the other?'

'No, mate. I've had enough roundabout excitement for one day. Save it for tomorrow.'

From the first garage after leaving the interstate from Salt Lake City to Tooele, we purchased a crate of lager for the evening and, after discovering that Utah law caps alcoholic content at 3.2 per cent, bought another.

Lee is the proud owner of a black Trans-Am (almost identical to the one used in *Knight Rider*, minus the red fairy lights at the front) and before we cracked the crates open he took us for a quick Trans-Am experience. A wheel spin that filled the air with a distinct smell of rubber, acceleration up a road behind his apartment and a handbrake skid later, Bateman and I found ourselves back outside Lee's apartment in less than two minutes and wanting a Trans-Am ourselves.

Sitting on their balcony whilst making short work of the lager, I produced the book of laws and proceeded to explain, once again, how I was intending to spend my summer.

'So, how are you going to hunt for a whale in landlocked Utah?' asked Lee, referring to my next goal.

'Simple. I'm going to hire a boat at a lake somewhere and, as long as I'm at least trying to hunt a whale, surely the law has been broken.'

We drank into the evening and I tried to steer the conversation away from my crime spree. I turned to face Jen.

'So have you lived here all your life then, Jen?' I asked. She shook her head confidently, removing the bottle from her lips.

'No. I was born in Georgia, then my mom and I moved to Montana because she met a guy there. Then his grandparents died and we inherited their house in Iowa so we moved there. Then my mom died so I moved to Florida to be with my aunt before moving back to Montana to be with my grandma. Then back to Florida to be with a guy who ended up going to Japan with the navy and then the person I was staying with turned psychotic so I moved to Kentucky to be with my dad but it didn't work out so I moved to Utah where I met Lee and we got a place together.'

'Oh. That's a no then.'

We continued drinking on their balcony into the early hours. The absurdly low alcohol content had resulted in eighteen empty cans of Budweiser at my feet alone and shortly before two in the morning I decided it was time for bed. I had a whale to hunt the next day and I left Bateman and Lee still talking as I made my way to the apartment's spare room. No sooner had my head hit the pillow than I was soothed to sleep by the sound of Lee throwing up in the bathroom opposite.

It had been four days since my illicit card game with Arden in Globe, and when I woke up I was desperate to break a law which would take my overall record above 50 per cent. Bateman and I headed back towards Salt Lake City.

Among the initial press coverage before I left home, I had read a story written by a man called Matthew D.

LaPlante who worked for the *Salt Lake Tribune*. Unlike the others, LaPlante's report was not at all in favour of what I was doing and instead suggested I should reconsider my criminal itinerary in Salt Lake City. The reason for this was that he had contacted legal experts who had found no law banning the hunting of whales in the state (which I had used as an example when explaining my plan to the reporters). However, later in the article, the state Division of Wildlife Resources spokesman Mark Hadley informed the reader that 'the federal Marine Mammal Protection Act makes it illegal for any person residing in the United States to kill any marine mammal – anywhere'. The last time I checked a map of the US, Utah was still one of its fifty states and therefore somewhere where it was illegal to hunt marine mammals. Tenuous, but it was good enough for my purposes.

After finding a suitable nearby lake that had boats available for hire, I booked one for later on in the evening when Lee and Jen would have finished work. In the meantime, Bateman and I had another day in which to prep the hardware. Wal-Mart, a huge American department store, was a stone's throw away from Lee's house in Tooele and seemed the perfect place to purchase the supplies – even if I had to put them together myself. One of Lee's butter knives, a roll of duct tape and a 98-cent broom (after the head had been unceremoniously snapped off) made an ideal spear and something a *Blue Peter* presenter would be proud of if they ever decided to show children how to make sub-par hunting equipment. I was ready to roll.

Our target, Jordanelle State Park, lies thirty miles east of Salt Lake City and contains the Jordanelle Reservoir, where the hunt would take place. This was not so much because of the likelihood of finding a heavyweight mammal as the fact that the Great Salt Lake smells funny and we didn't want to have to spend a day there. As we arrived and surveyed the beauty of the park, the choice of lake seemed to be approved by all ... until they saw the selection of boats.

'What boat have you hired, Rich?' enquired Bateman. 'It had better not be one of those pieces of shit there,' he added, pointing disapprovingly at a row of four-seaters.

'Well, I went for the cheapest so it probably is one of them,' I replied, smirking at my own stinginess.

'You tight bastard!' yelled Bateman, reading my expression perfectly. 'I'm not getting in that crap. I'm hiring a jet ski.'

'You can't,' I snapped. 'We've passed their hiring times. I only got this because I asked really nicely for an extra half-hour.'

Bateman eventually acceded and all four of us waited on the small wooden jetty for our boat to be driven round to us. To Bateman's dismay, the vessel which docked was indeed one of the 'pieces of shit' he had so eloquently described. We clambered in and were each handed a lifejacket which had been lying in the murky brown water that covered the bottom of the boat.

'You don't have to use it but it's nice to have if you need to,' remarked the assistant helpfully to Jen, who was already convinced we weren't coming out of this alive.

'Any chance of encountering some whales in the lake?' I asked jokingly.

'Nah. Should see plenty of driftwood though.' He quickly talked me through the controls of the motor and the rules of the lake. The 'no wake' zone which surrounded the jetty meant that speeds were to be kept to less than five miles per hour until we were a safe distance away from the area. I was then shown the choke, the throttle, gears and emergency stop and as soon as he allowed us to leave forgot the lot, stalling the engine as I tried to pull away. The second attempt went more smoothly, and as our 13-horse-power engine propelled us painstakingly slowly away from the jetty I wondered why I was even informed of the speed limit at all.

'You have to be the one to do it. You're American,' I said to Jen, handing her the spear I had so beautifully prepared. Jen took the weapon in one hand, raising the other to her forehead and looking across the lake into the sun's rays. She seemed as if she was taking her role seriously, holding the spear and gritting her teeth whilst we took photos for posterity – she demanded several be taken in case her hair or posture wasn't to her liking.

'Let's go swimming,' suggested Lee, who had already taken his shirt off in preparation. Bateman agreed and also removed his shirt, sending the boat into a swaying frenzy as he launched himself into the lake's deep, clear water.

It was obvious we were never going to kill a whale in the lake but the wording of the law meant that Jen and I had to hunt for one and that simply meant searching. I soon felt we had done this satisfactorily, and with forty-five minutes of hire time remaining Lee took over at the motor. The lack of whales must have had an effect on him and he turned his attention to a crane which kept appearing, causing him to send the boat unexpectedly lurching in all directions as he attempted to run over it.

When the sun dropped below the pastoral hills which surrounded the lake we pointed the boat in the direction of the jetty and headed back towards the land. We still had twenty minutes to go but with the speed of the engine we all agreed jokingly that it probably wasn't enough time to get back.

On the return car journey, Jen invited us to stay for another night but was interrupted by a roadkill game first.

'Moving roadkill,' Bateman remarked observantly. 'A deer.' A pick-up truck had overtaken us and in the back lay the remains of a doe. 'Surely that's a game winner?'

'I don't know,' I replied, wondering what the road-kill judging panel would say if such a thing existed.

'Moving roadkill is bloody good, though.' (We later decided a dinosaur would be considered 'ultimate roadkill').

'So are you going to stay another night?' Jen repeated.

'Don't many people stay round yours, then?' I asked inquisitively.

'One of Lee's friends did once but he tried to have sex with me.'

'Oh.'

'You gonna stay then?'

How could we refuse? Motels weren't cheap, we were starting to get to know Salt Lake City like the back of our hands and staying with Jen and Lee was a joy. As a result, Lee suggested we all hit the booze again that night and go to a club in town.

What a great idea, I thought. As far as the laws went I was now four and three (as American sports fans say) and in need of a celebration. The hunt, along with my criminal actions in Indian Wells and Globe, meant that I had broken three laws in a row and the successes had a lead of one over the failures. I may not have killed a marine mammal in the lake today but I was definitely ready to party and, as Lee so nicely put it, was ready to 'go out and do some proper whale hunting!'

7

Cheesed Off

The morning began with my fourth hangover of the trip so far and the disturbing revelation that Bateman was still only on his second pair of boxer shorts.

'Yeah, they'll do,' he remarked as he held the garment to his nose to inhale the pant-like aroma. 'If not, I can always go back to using the first pair anyway.'

The talk of underwear reminded me that I had a cheese factory to ring, and I headed to Tooele library to make the all-important call.

Throughout the entire state of South Dakota, it is illegal for anyone to lie down and fall asleep in a cheese factory. Why this should be I wasn't entirely sure, but I could only assume that a terrible accident had once occurred after someone had dozed off. It was one of the very first laws I'd chosen to include on the

99

trip as it was one of my favourites and was as bizarre as they got. The problem I faced was that I had already sent numerous emails to the Valley Queen cheese factory in the small South Dakotan town of Milbank. They hadn't replied to any of my requests to sleep in their factory and, even after I offered to work a shift in payment for the stay, had probably not regarded my inundations with the sincerity with which they were sent. Throwing caution to the wind, and considering no news was good news, I rang them anyway.

'Good morning. Valley Queen. Which department?'

'Um . . . I'm not really sure. I'm ringing to ask if I can stay in your cheese factory one night this week. Who would I have to speak to for that?'

'One moment please, sir.'

I waited while she patched me through to, most probably, the factory's resident psychiatrist, and eventually a genial-sounding lady came on the line. 'Mary speaking. How may I help you?'

I introduced myself, and told her what I was doing, why I was doing it and everything else that seemed pertinent before revealing the nature of my call. 'I'm ringing you because apparently it's illegal in the entire state of South Dakota to lie down and fall asleep in a cheese factory and I was wondering if there was any chance I could do so in yours.'

Mary sounded surprised. 'Well, I've never heard of that law before, but health and safety and state regulations mean there is no way you would be able to spend the night here.'

'Oh,' I replied, heartbroken. One of my favourite laws, shot down before I could even attempt it. 'So there's no way at all?' I asked, injecting a sense of panic and desperation into my voice.

'No.'

Now I was clutching at straws. 'How about if I just lay in the foyer with the security guard? That's in the factory, that'll count. He'll like me, I'm sure. We could tell each other all the things we've ever wanted to say but didn't have the time.'

'I'm sorry,' she replied firmly, before finishing with a closing note of clarification. 'I'm terribly sorry, but from the Valley Queen cheese factory and probably every factory in the state of South Dakota, it's a no.'

'Thanks anyway.'

So that was it. Another failure had reared its ugly head just when things were improving, but at least I didn't have to travel four hundred unnecessary miles to experience it. I felt a sudden loss in energy and slumped into a chair by the phone opposite two girls who had heard the entire conversation and were probably wondering if it was safe to talk to me. They stood up, walked a couple of steps towards me and then veered into an aisle, obviously deciding it wasn't in their best interest to begin a conversation. Alone in Tooele Public Library with a hangover from hell, caused, in part, by a girl who insisted we bought drinks that came in test tubes, I found myself back on 50 per cent and level terms once more.

I returned to Lee and Jen's and broke the news to

Bateman. He didn't seem too bothered by it and was still concerned about his boxer shorts dilemma, eventually playing it safe and remaining loyal to pair two.

The cheese factory was a bitter blow but its loss presented us with an open path to Chicago, one that didn't have to pass through South Dakota. I consulted the map and my bible of laws and turned quickly to Nebraska, Kansas, Iowa and Wyoming. Nothing. I couldn't believe it. I had the chance to change my entire route and visit four new states and there was no kind of stupid law that I could break. In Nebraska I had to be a parent, a daughter, a barber or a hotel owner to break any. In Marshalltown, Iowa I had to transform into a horse and eat a fire hydrant (neither of which I was too keen on), and a law in Newcastle, Wyoming decreed it was illegal for couples to have sex whilst standing inside a store's walk-in meat freezer. Even if I could find a willing girl, once inside the cramped conditions of a meat freezer I'm sure I wouldn't warm to her. Kansas had the only law by which I was tempted, but only for a second. In Natoma it was illegal to practise knife-throwing at men in striped suits. This law I would never attempt. I've never thrown a knife in my life and such is my hatred for pinstripes that I probably wouldn't be aiming to miss. I looked closer at the map. If I couldn't find a replacement, the next law waiting to be broken was in Chicago – almost 1,400 miles away.

*

Salt Lake City was starting to become very familiar to us, and as we drove from Tooele back into the city to meet Lee for lunch it was great not having to consult a map or ask for directions. The downtown area was sparse and never gridlocked and although many of the city streets comprised seven lanes of one-way traffic, the immaculately clean sidewalks and surrounding summer snow-topped mountains exuded a sense of freedom.

After joining him at the tail-end of his lunch break, I explained to Lee that we were no longer in a hurry to leave after the cheese factory had refused permission and he asked if we wanted to stay for a further night. On the understanding that we didn't drink and condemn him to another hangover and that it was OK with Jen, we accepted and left Lee to return to work as we tried to kill some more time and get ourselves a bite to eat.

A visit to the nearby Arby's restaurant seemed appropriate. We thought it would be rude not to try all the fast food chains at least once and Arby's, which specializes in roast beef sandwiches, was now added to the list of the ones we had visited. Although the restaurant stood alongside the likes of Burger King and Denny's, what was of more interest to me was what stood alongside this actual building. Friday seemed a strange day to open a store but the sign suggested it was indeed the 'Grand Opening' of Dollar Tree and, with my love for British pound shops, I jumped at the chance to visit what seemed to be an

American version. The electric doors took for ever to open and I stepped inside, taking a deep breath. It smelled exactly like they do in Britain – a musky smell of tat.

'Breathe it in, Bateman. Breathe it in.'

The trouble with American shops is that their price tags lie. Different states have a different amount of sales tax to add to different products so these are tallied up at the checkout. In the US, a child who has a dollar in his pocket to buy sweets must add the total up in his head before adding the appropriate tax and then working out if he has enough or deciding what he has to put back. Utah's sales tax stands at 4.75 per cent making this a $1.05 shop, not a dollar shop as the sign suggested. This, however, didn't matter to me. My mind was thinking of pounds and pence and I quickly had my brain working hard on the case. If this was a $1.05 shop then, at the current exchange rate, it was a 58p shop! My heart was pounding. This was exciting. If the telephone call earlier in the morning had been disheartening, this experience was definitely making up for it. Rows of deodorants stood juxtaposed with packs of twenty scouring pads; tasteless bags and handheld electric fans were sitting in baskets in plentiful supply and the toy section was full of blatantly cheap replications of well-known games with unimaginative titles such as 'Mega 4-In-A-Row' and 'Who's Who?' It was brilliant.

We had already bought Lee and Jen their weekly shop and copious amounts of alcohol as payment for our stay but the invitation to stay one more night gave me the idea of buying them leaving presents. We decided we would get them matching armbands which they could use that evening in the communal swimming pool they shared with their fifty or so neighbours, together with one other present each. We split up in search of that special gift for our respective recipient (I was buying for Lee, and Bateman was shopping for Jen) and reconvened at the checkout ten minutes later with presents in hand before finally leaving the shop. As the door swung open it hit a vending machine, which I noticed sold the *Salt Lake Tribune*. Wondering what Mr LaPlante was moaning about this week, I spent little time in pondering and quickly produced two quarters from my wallet and bought a copy. We returned to the car and I began to flick through the pages, searching for the name. The national and local pages featured no article by him and nor did the sport, lifestyle or any of the other sections of the paper. After I had read a couple of uninteresting local stories, it was ingeniously recycled as wrapping paper for our gifts. The armbands were deceptively tricky to wrap but the twelve by four-inch sock ironing board I had bought Lee was much simpler. Bateman, who had decided to use most of the remaining duct tape to adequately secure the presents, was having a much easier time with a framed picture he had bought depicting a couple having a wonderful time on a yacht – a gift we hoped Jen would hang on her wall as a fond reminder of our whale-hunting experience.

Back in Tooele, gifts unwrapped and graciously accepted by our hosts, we all went for a swim in the pool – unfortunately without the frog and tiger armbands. Upon our return to their apartment I explained the situation the cheese factory had left me in and Jen took the book of laws, flicking straight to the Iowa page.

'What about this one?' she asked, pointing at the law which states that it's illegal for any kiss to last longer than five minutes. 'Why don't you break that? I used to live there; I could get someone to do it.'

'Could you?' I asked, sounding pathetically desperate. 'I looked at the law but didn't really think twice about it. Easily doable?'

'Should be. Most of my friends are pregnant, though.'

Jen explained that she used to live in a small town called Fontanelle and, after showing it to me on the map, assured me of success.

The following day was the beginning of our second week in America and there was nothing to celebrate. Fontanelle was over a thousand miles away, Chicago even further, and after three enjoyable days in Salt Lake City it was time to say our goodbyes to Lee and Jen. I left the three-in-one electronic instrument as a final gift for our hosts and we made our way downtown for the last time. Lee's house can't be more than ten miles from Salt Lake City but the fact that it stands on the other side of a colossal hill, reminiscent of the

Scottish Highlands, almost doubles the distance you have to drive. Taking a wrong turn and heading towards a tiny set of houses, we passed a roundabout. This must have been the second one of which Lee had spoken and I had found it completely serendipitously. Either that or Salt Lake City was the roundabout capital of America. Say whatever you want about the Mormon religion, they make a bloody good traffic circle.

We finally said goodbye to Lee at Salt Lake Motorsports, then Bateman and I returned to the car and joined I-80, a road on which we would remain for the following week and the next 1,500 miles until our arrival in Chicago.

After only ten miles, the densely packed interstate roads which surround Salt Lake City petered out as the road began to climb into the mountains and away from urbanization. It's on these roads where driving in America really becomes a nuisance. The six-laners which are bountiful in the cities give way to just two and a simple glance out of the window can be life-threatening, as taking your eyes off the road can result in hitting one of the shreds of truck tyres which litter the blacktop in their hundreds. Overtaking is also a major problem. Drivers' failure to pull over when we were behind them was getting Bateman annoyed, and the fact that they left their cars in cruise control and began overtaking at a speed which was only a mere fraction faster than the rate at which the over-takee was travelling made the entire operation a long, drawn-out affair that seemed to take an eternity to complete. And there was little roadkill. New games we devised just didn't keep us enthralled but we did begin to count the number of carriages in passing trains. A 75 was followed by a 68, then an 82 and finally a record-breaking 107. Like I said, it wasn't enthralling and little happened until we entered Wyoming.

'ROADKILL!' shouted Bateman. 'It was a bear! I'm sure of it,' he added.

'Shut up,' I snapped. 'It couldn't have been a bear.'

'It bloody was. It was massive.'

'What kind of bear, then?'

'I dunno, it didn't have a head. It was a mysterious headless monster.'

The roads were becoming clearer and much less cluttered as we made our way through Wyoming, and with no one around us Bateman increased our speed to well above the strictly enforced 75 mph speed limit, a welcome way to get through the dull drive. Suddenly the flashing of lights and the wail of a state trooper's siren behind gave us a highlight in an otherwise uneventful day. Not wanting to be struck by the fast-moving interstate traffic the official made his way to my side of the vehicle.

'Do you know why I've stopped you, sir?' he asked after I'd wound down my window and generously greeted him.

'Maybe I was going a bit too fast,' Bateman admitted.

'A bit fast? Ninety-seven in a seventy-five limit. I clocked you whilst I was driving the other way. Can you join me in my car, please?'

As Bateman accepted the trooper's invitation, I used the car's rear-view mirror to follow the actions taking place behind me. The entire ticket-writing seemed friendly enough; the state trooper sat and talked as if he'd known Bateman for years and Bateman sat at ease, hardly fazed by the double-barrelled shotgun which sat alongside him.

'What happened?' I asked as Bateman returned to the car.

'Two hundred and twenty dollar fine.' Bateman smirked proudly. 'Gonna take that home and frame it. If I don't pay it, a warrant will be released for my arrest in a month's time.'

'You gonna pay it, then?' I asked.

'Bollocks am I. Two hundred and twenty dollars! That guy said if I don't pay it, I won't be allowed to leave the country.'

'He was bluffing, I reckon.'

'Yeah, that's what I reckon. And look, he spelled the name of my town wrong. I live in Redruth not Redroof like he's written. I reckon that's void.'

'I don't think that voids the offence, Bateman.'

'Don't care if it doesn't, I ain't paying it. It's just a good job he didn't clock me ten minutes ago. I was doing about a hundred and twenty.'

So the two-week anniversary was something to celebrate after all: Bateman had joined me in law-breaking. Before today, he had been the official photographer and had been present at all the law-breakings, but had never actually broken one himself. He even passed up the opportunity to peel an orange in California. Now, after only one law, he had super-seded me. He'd been warned by a law enforcer and threatened with arrest. Lucky bastard. In a month's time, Bateman could be a fugitive. We liked the thought of that.

Still hundreds of miles short of Fontanelle, Bateman had single-handedly brought the laws back to five out of nine, restoring the successes' slender lead. As we made our way to our motel for the night the I-80 felt less like a long and tiresome road to Chicago and more like the road to recovery.

8

Missing and Kissing

For the second time on the holiday I woke to find myself fully dressed, television still on and no Bateman. We had definitely both checked into the Oak Grove Inn in the Nebraskan town of Grand Island (which was neither grand nor an island – not even a peninsula) but now he had vanished and his bed appeared to have been slept in by the entire contents of his suitcase. I began to retrace our steps from last night in my head to figure out where he could be, and took a walk to the lake which was situated at the foot of our room's patio door. The previous night had begun in the bar next to the motel and we had arrived too late for a meal. That I could remember. The half-empty pizza box I found by the television on my return to the room was a major clue. The fact that it was a jalapeño pizza was the giveaway and, although I lacked a deerstalker hat and magnifying glass, I was on the case.

We had left the pool table after I lost every game we played, returned to the bar and started talking to a man about American sports. I remembered saying that baseball was just rounders, American football shouldn't be called football at all and basketball was the worst game ever invented. Luckily for my face, he seemed to agree and we spent most of the evening talking about soccer, which I eventually drummed into him was the real football. Then I ordered the pizzas, allowing one of the barmaids to choose one of the toppings. I hate jalapeños and would never have chosen them and nor would Bateman, who, I remembered, didn't order anything. He had left me in the bar and gone to the attached club, which was called Voodoo. I was meant to join him but for some reason I had returned in a merry state to the motel and watched the US Open of Professional Eating. All the excitement of the spaghetti Bolognese round must have sent me to sleep fully clothed, leaving the biggest piece of the jigsaw still missing – the whereabouts of Bateman.

Checkout time was eleven and at ten forty-five, after a shower, I explained to the desk clerk that I would love to check out but couldn't, owing to the fact that Bateman's room key was still in his possession. Thirty minutes passed, and after packing the suitcases into the car and perusing the *Grand Island Independent* provided in the foyer, I took a walk to the club to check that his body wasn't lying in a ditch somewhere outside the front doors. It wasn't.

As midday approached, all manner of scenarios raced through my head from the simple to the absurd. I couldn't imagine why he would want to take off with the travelling circus without telling me, and how on earth I was going to explain to his mother that a pack of hungry wolves had viciously butchered him on the fifty-yard walk back to the motel. If Bateman was dead, I thought, he could have had the decency to wait until we had reached Georgia, where it's a crime to swear in front of a dead body whilst it is lying in a funeral home or coroner's office. At least in death he would have been helping the cause and doing me a favour by taking one for the team. In my eyes he would have been a martyr, a saviour for the common criminal. On the other hand, he was probably just waking up in his cell with a court appearance date looming. From my point of view, that wouldn't have been too bad either and seemed to be the odds on favourite explanation for the time being. Everything fitted the story – he wouldn't have known the motel's number and therefore wouldn't have been able to use his one phone call and they would just be releasing him now, ready to return him to the foyer. He was fast becoming a better law-breaker than me. In the meantime, I was in serious danger of having to pay for an additional night as the desk clerk was beginning to look impatient at my unwillingness to leave. We still hadn't vacated the room, though I wasn't too worried about having to pack Bateman's boxer shorts myself since I knew most of them had never been worn.

Minutes later an old and battered town car pulled up outside the motel with Bateman in the passenger seat and a small dog perched on the back seat. The fact that the car had neither siren nor lights and was driven by a woman was the giveaway that he had not spent the night in jail, and the night's sleep had been somewhere much more comfortable than a cell.

'Where the hell have you been?' I asked quite loudly. 'Checkout time was over an hour ago.'

Bateman's eyes were glazed over and his hair was scruffy, but he was able to produce a reasonable explanation of the events which had unfolded.

'After the club, I got into some car and went to a party. There was this house with a big, angry dog tied up and there was plenty of beer so I was happy. Then we all got kicked out and some guy told me a story about a shooting. Then I went back to some old bird's house. Her name was Crystal. Never did stop taking the piss out of that name.'

'Right. Anyway, we're ready to go.'

Fontanelle was now well within our sights and we turned south off the interstate onto the N72, which would hopefully carry us the twenty or so miles to the town. After no more than a mile the small, single lane roads with endless fields either side made us feel as if interstate travel was a million miles away and we were as good as nowhere. At every crossroad the N72 met up with a road as straight and true as our own and we could see that the grid pattern which features in most of America's cities was being replicated on a grander and more rural scale. As our road descended into the rolling green pastures and rose to reveal more of the same, a sign to Fontanelle was visible and we took the required right onto a road which fluctuated over the fields and plains but remained firmly and eternally at ninety degrees to the road we had just left and exactly parallel to the roads which sprouted from other junctions. I looked at the map and discovered that most roads in America's Midwest are like this. With simple, open land in every direction, road-builders had no obstacles to avoid and simply laid them straight, leaving the map looking like the layout of a circuit board or the pipeline screensaver I once had on my computer.

The 675 people who live in Fontanelle must like living there but from my first impressions of the town I can't think why. It sits in the middle of a collection of huge fields in the middle of a state in the middle of the country. In whatever direction you chose to leave, you'd be presented with the same thing – nothing. It may not have been an Arizonan desert town, miles from civilization and yards from cacti, but to me, Fontanelle, a speck amongst meadows and endless, flat greenery, was just as isolated. I parked the car and entered the single shop, which was located on Main Street – a totally undeserved and unjustified title which made a mockery of other Main Streets around the world. Quickly taking four quarters out of my wallet, I walked over to the pay phone and rang Lee.

'Hello?' shouted Lee over the noise of car engines.

'Where are you to?' I asked.

'At the race track. Where are you?' he replied without the 'to'. This new American accent of his must have removed all the Cornishisms in him.

'In Fontanelle. Eventually. You should see this place. My God. Can we get this thing over and done with, please? Where's Jen?'

'She's at home. Ring me back in about forty-five minutes and she'll sort it out for you.'

'Right. I'll try to amuse myself until then,' I replied confidently. 'I'll check out the sights.'

Forty-five minutes was going to be hard to pass in a town of this size but as I returned to the car and placed the key in the ignition I was sure that a slow and detailed look round the town would do the trick. Jen had told me that the shop was the hub of the town and judging by the three people who were in the vicinity at the moment today was no exception. We pulled out slowly onto Main Street and instantly passed an old, shabby hut on our right which turned out to be Fontanelle Town Hall. A quick right revealed the town's water tower and, in the house immediately after landmark number two, we were presented with the highlight of our self-guided tour – a man who had converted his garage into a bar and seemed to be enjoying every moment of his lonesome debauchery. Another corner and we were back on Main Street and pulling into the parking space we had vacated four minutes earlier.

Thirty long minutes later and my impatience sent me back into the shop to phone Lee again.

'Hi, Lee. Any luck with Jen and her mates?' I asked.

'Not really, mate. She's tried a few but they all say no.'

'I don't blame them. They must have seen a picture of me somehow.'

'Just go out on the street and find one,' Lee suggested.

'Lee, have you actually been to Fontanelle? There is nothing and no one here. It's awful. How could Jen have lived here?'

'Right, I'm handing you over to Jen.'

'I've tried a few numbers but no one seems to be up for it. Loads of them are pregnant, remember?' said Jen as she took to the phone.

'OK, but the only reason I'm here is because of you,' I replied, pressuring Jen for success.

Suddenly the phone went dead and when I held the phone close to my ear I could hear nothing. Just as I was about to hang up, a phone ring could be heard down the receiver.

'You still there?' asked Jen.

'Yeah. What're we doing? How can the phone be ringing? Is this like a three-way call or something?' I asked frantically as the phone was answered and the ringing ceased.

'Yes. Now shush and let me talk.'

I listened in absolute silence as Jen spoke to the mother of one of her old friends, Erin. I heard that Erin's mother didn't know her daughter's new number and so the conversation ended.

'You still there, Rich?' Jen asked.

'Yep. What we gonna do?'

'No worry. It's easy. Just pop round to my other friend Tanya's house. She'll do it.'

'Is she pregnant?' I enquired.

'Um. Yes, I think so. OK, I'll give you the address, then all you have to do is speak to her mother . . .'

It dawned on me that this really wasn't going to work.

'Her mother? What am I going to say to her? Hiya, you don't know me but can I kiss your daughter for more than five minutes because it's illegal to in Iowa? No way. That would be the action of a madman,' I snapped. 'Don't you know anyone else?'

'Nope, sorry. Everyone's changed their numbers or don't want to know.'

'OK then. Thanks anyway.'

Another failure. But the first about which I didn't feel any remorse or disappointment. Failure here meant I was free to leave Fontanelle which was definitely not a negative, and I felt as liberated as Patrick McGoohan after escaping Portmeirion in the final episode of *The Prisoner*. Fontanelle, I remembered, was the name given to the soft spot on a baby's head – no wonder everyone there seemed to be pregnant.

Back on the I-80, and after Bateman had spotted a dead deer on the side of the road, meaning I definitely did need a dinosaur in order to win the game, we pulled over at a bar for an evening meal.

The Sportts Bar (yes, two ts) was as typical of an American restaurant as it gets. Tables situated by the windows seemed attached to the walls and most definitely part of them. Seating was made up of straight, leather-covered, plastic bolsters which meant a shuffle down to the end of the row was required. The most interesting item on the menu was the 2lb Sumo Burger Challenge. It was mighty tempting to try to win the T-shirt that was on offer if you were able to finish it, and a much better prospect than the rather cheap Cup-a-soup of the day. Behind us sat seven men, all dressed in regulation baseball caps, jeans and checked shirts, looking like extras from *The Dukes of Hazzard*. I glanced back at the menu. It wasn't a Friday, but I had missed too many Friday Fish 'n' Chips days whilst over in America and although I was here for a crime spree that was one law I wasn't happy to be breaking. Fish and chips it would have to be.

When I was paying for the meal at the counter I couldn't help asking the cashier, who had her hair in a bun with a pencil pushed through it (all that was missing was the jug of coffee in her hand and the cigarette hanging from her mouth as she asked if I wanted a top-up), why the word Sportts was spelt with two ts.

'Was it a typo by the signwriter and then you had to label everything with it?' I asked.

The waitress looked puzzled. 'No, it's just a name that sticks in your head,' she replied.

It was a typo.

Chicago was growing ever nearer and the I-80 carried us over the mighty Mississippi River into Illinois. We had officially entered eastern America. No doubt gently sloped, tree-covered hills met the riverbanks and the Mississippi's broad, encompassing presence appeared dominating and powerful, but I was aware of none of this. An earlier 'Deer – Next 10 Miles' sign meant that my eyes were firmly glued to the road. Being so far behind in the roadkill game, it was eyes down for a full house.

9

American Brother-in-Law

Bateman lives four miles from my home. While I live in a coastal village, he lives in the closest town, Redruth. For many years now, the 'Welcome to Redruth' sign has stated that the town is twinned with a place called Mineral Point in Wisconsin. I have always promised myself that if I were ever within a hundred miles of Mineral Point at any time – not thinking it anything but a very remote possibility – then I would drop in to visit. To Mineral Point from Madison, where we stopped for the night, was under fifty miles, which seemed like nothing by now. We had a couple of spare days due to the cheese factory fiasco and it seemed very unbrotherly of us to not visit our twin when we were so close.

Strangely lettered roads led the way to Mineral Point after we left the interstate, and things began to get very confusing. The K road was followed by the HHH, the QQ and the G. Eventually, sticking to properly signposted roads which hadn't been selected by Carol Vorderman, we arrived in Mineral Point and parked on what appeared to be the main street. I stepped out of the car and surveyed my surroundings, looking for telltale signs of similarities between Redruth and this small town in south-west Wisconsin. I didn't see too many. Mineral Point was deathly quiet, old ladies weren't talking to each other in the road, and I couldn't see a single kebab or charity shop. The street, which we later discovered was called High Street, was similar in size to Redruth's Fore Street and contained no more than fifty or so storefronts. We slowly made our way down the sidewalk in order to find the local information centre. We passed what seemed to be an astronomically large number of antique shops and galleries, far more than you'd expect to survive in a town of only three thousand residents, and many, many times more than you'd see in Redruth, where the closest thing you get to art is the profanity scrawled on the side of a boarded-up building by a miscreant who had smashed the windows a few weeks before. After only a minute of walking, as we neared the halfway mark of High Street, I stopped the only person in sight and asked her for directions.

'Excuse me; we're from Redruth, and—' The mere mention of the word sent the woman into a hand-shaking frenzy. She gripped my hand with more strength than I would have believed someone of her age and size could muster.

'Oh, really? Very pleased to meet you. Welcome to Mineral Point,' she replied, still shaking my hand in what appeared to be an attempt to break it off to keep as a souvenir.

'Thanks. I was wondering if you could tell us where the local information centre is?' I asked, hoping her shaking hand was also her pointing one too.

'The Chamber of Commerce right there,' she replied, indicating a building only thirty yards from us and thankfully releasing my right hand from its vigorous roller-coaster ride of a shake. 'Yeah, Joy'll help you out with all you need to know.'

We thanked the lady and made our way across the road to the Mineral Point Chamber of Commerce. Joy Gieseke, as her card explained, was the executive director of the Chamber and was just as pleased to meet us as the lady in the street had been – minus the handshake ordeal. Courtesy of Joy and her abundant array of brochures and information booklets, I began to learn much more about Mineral Point. The Redruth connection stems from the town's mining heritage. The discovery of lead gave rise to the 'mineral rush' and prospectors flocked to the town, including settlers who came from as far afield as Cornwall. The town's Cornish links are visible to this day in the limestone and sandstone buildings constructed by the early immigrants. Most of Joy's brochures seemed to feature Pendarvis Mine as Mineral Point's main attraction. Pendarvis was also the name of a tin mine just miles from my home and Joy, noticing my interest in the site tour, handed me a piece of pink paper.

'That's a free ticket for the tour. Sorry, I only have one,' she said, turning to Bateman. 'So what's Redruth like?'

Bateman and I stared at each other, both wondering what the polite and euphemistic way of saying 'shithole' was. Bateman's brain must have clicked.

'Well, it's better than Camborne. That's just full of teenage pregnancies . . .'

'. . . and yobs,' I added, hoping that painting a crude picture of Camborne might make Joy think highly of her twin town.

'Well, we've had some of the kids over here. The high schools do an exchange every few years or so. They seem to enjoy it,' remarked Joy, who was clearly playing it safe as well.

'Talking of Camborne, does Mineral Point have any local rivals, like Redruth has Camborne?' Bateman asked.

'Well, there's always been a rivalry with Dodgeville just down the road.'

'Speaking as Cornishmen, they shall be our enemy too, then,' I said.

We sat down at a handsome oak table in the centre of the room and Joy produced a map to show us more of Mineral Point and where we would have to go for the Pendarvis tour. I was fascinated by the layout of the town.

'It's not a grid pattern,' I said, with maybe too much excitement, knowing most town maps resemble potato waffles.

'Yeah, we're very proud of that here,' Joy replied.

'It's a wonderful random mess of roads. It's great. No roundabouts, though.' Maybe the fascination with roundabouts was beginning to grow into a slight obsession.

'I love roundabouts,' Joy replied with a smile on her face, leaving me wondering if my condition was contagious. 'There's one in Dodgeville, I believe.'

'Is there?' I replied in surprise, instantly ruing the pact I had made to hate Dodgeville just seconds before.

We remained in the Chamber for quite some time, learning bizarre facts about our twin town. The state's nickname 'the Badger State' was first conceived in this area, after early settlers' crude shelters which were known as 'badger holes'; the town had lost by a single vote to Madison to become Wisconsin's state capital; and more than fifty artists, artisans, authors, musicians and performing artists reside in Mineral Point. Bateman and I, however, were interested in more important matters.

'Is there anywhere we can get a pasty?' I asked.

'Well, the Red Rooster is only just down the road. I've heard they make very nice pasties.'

Bateman and I simply scoffed at her suggestion.

'We'll be the judges of that,' we said in almost perfect unison. 'Much as I like you, Joy, I can't take an American's advice on what a good pasty is,' I added jokingly.

'After you've been there, come back here and I'll introduce you to Carole Rule and her husband. Norman is probably one of the most Cornish people in Mineral Point, I would imagine.'

I wondered what she meant by that. Following Joy's directions, Bateman and I took another walk down the empty main street of the town and meandered along to the door of the Red Rooster, where renovation work was currently in progress. Scaffolding and ladders were propped up against the wall and the entire town's population seemed to be enjoying a meal inside.

Petrol, fast food and nearly everything else might be cheaper in America, but pasties certainly aren't. Grudgingly, I searched for five dollars in my wallet. A pasty is as quintessentially Cornish as mining and fishing, and as there was certainly no coast off which to catch a couple of mackerel by Mineral Point, I was desperate to experience the nearest thing to true Cornish heritage I could hope to find here. I ordered my food and waited with bated breath, but when the pasty finally arrived I made some rather disturbing discoveries. First, it came in a polystyrene box not a bag. Second, I had been presented with a fork with which to eat it. Furthermore, after lifting the lid to judge the pasty on its presentation, I discovered it had no crimp and resembled a deflated scone. Last, and most alarming, a polystyrene condiment container was then handed to me.

'And here's your chilli sauce, sir,' said the waitress quite cheerfully.

'My what? Did you say chilli sauce? What do I want that for?' I pushed the container back along the counter in her direction. 'How dare you,' I added in jest.

But the proof of the pasty is, of course, in the eating. I picked it up out of its box and took a bite. Bateman looked on expectantly. 'What's it like?'

'Um ... different,' I replied. It wasn't so much the ingredients that were wrong; it was the texture and the taste. It was dry and quite stodgy and I almost regretted declining the chilli sauce – a difficult thing for a Cornishman to admit. Disappointed, and still very hungry, we returned to the Chamber of Commerce.

'How was it?' Joy asked upon our entry.

'Don't ask,' I replied without expression.

Just as she promised, Joy led us across the road to the local estate agent's, run by Carole and Norman Rule. Rule is a very Cornish name, and I had very high expectations as we entered the office of the Mineral Point branch of the ERA Arthur Real Estate & Appraisals. Norman Rule was an elderly gentleman in a tartan shirt and glasses; his wife was charming, incredibly affable and very welcoming, and turned out to be the woman I had accosted in the street earlier.

'Ah, I believe we've met before,' I said, keeping my hands where I could see them (I'd learned my lesson).

The office was small and clean, leading me to deduce that real estate wasn't a hasty, relentless business in Mineral Point. The walls were covered with maps and pictures of Cornwall which might have even outnumbered the house advertisements in the front window. I pointed on a map to where I was from before questioning Norman on his Cornishness. His ancestors, he explained, were originally from Camborne and Redruth and came to Mineral Point among the first prospectors during the 'mineral rush' of which I had earlier learned.

Joy, who had obviously forgotten about her responsibilities in the Chamber of Commerce, suggested after about fifteen minutes that we should have a picture taken outside of us all. We made our way out of the estate agent's with an entourage which had grown almost to procession level, and sat in front of one of the numerous antique shops in the High Street while Carole captured the moment with Joy's camera.

Returning with Joy to the Chamber, we asked where we could buy a Cornish flag for our car. Sentiment was reaching the surface, and the Chrysler's featureless parcel shelf needed a bit of Cornish embellishment. If we were ever going to find such a thing in America, this would be the place to look.

'I'll ring Catherine for you, but I'm not sure if she's open,' Joy said.

'But it's one o'clock on a Tuesday afternoon,' I replied incredulously. The telephone was never answered and we learned that the only shop in the US where a Cornish flag could be purchased opens every day of the week except Tuesdays.

'You could always try the tour shop. They might have some,' Joy suggested.

Using the map Joy had given us, we made our way to the Pendarvis tour shop and amidst the copious amount of Cornish paraphernalia, from pencils to mugs, that adorned its shelves we did find a small Cornish flag and a Union Jack. With both attached to the car's aerial, we returned to the centre of town along Shake Rag Street, where traditional Cornish cottages stood at the foot of hills which had once been dotted with lead mines. The road was tiny and placid and if it weren't for the torturous heat would have definitely reminded me of home. We left the car by the side of the road while we took a quick photo, and noticed a huge Cornish flag hanging at the entrance to the Mineral Point Living Arts Center.

'Ask if we can buy theirs off them,' shouted Bateman, who was still intent on decorating the parcel shelf. Thinking it was a great idea, I entered the building and walked straight into a meeting.

'Sorry to interrupt you but I was wondering if your Cornish flag was for sale and if I could buy it off you. The shop which sells them is shut.' Pleasant folks, they weren't the least bit annoyed that I had interrupted a meeting and were keen to learn about my trip around the States.

'I'll ring Catherine,' said one of the ladies as she rose from her chair and made her way into the office where I was standing.

'I think you'll find she's not in,' I said rather smugly, remembering the earlier phone call Joy had made. I turned my attention back to the other ladies round the table and got ready to make an offer on their flag. Surely thirty dollars would seal the deal.

The other lady returned. 'She's gonna be there in ten minutes and open the shop especially for you,' she said.

'Oh . . . thanks.'

Catherine Whitford's shop was called the Cornish Corner. As Catherine approached from the dark interior to unlock the door, I apologized profusely for the interruption to her day off and thanked her for opening just for me and at such short notice.

'Oh, that doesn't matter. Tekter and I only live in the house out the back. It's not far to walk.'

Trehawke's Prince Tekter (to give him his full name) is Catherine's six-year-old shih-tzu, who scuttled about sniffing at my legs while Catherine showed me round the store. Cornish plates, tin products imported from St Just and a fine selection of pewter, tin and sterling silver jewellery featured in a consummate collection of everything Cornish. Catherine's family name, Trehawke, she explained, dates back in Cornwall as far as the reign of William the Conqueror and features within the pages of the Domesday Book. I made my way towards the shelf where the Cornish flags were stacked.

'So how much is that massive flag there?' I asked.

Catherine looked at me dolefully. 'Well, they're quite expensive. I have to import them in from overseas. That big one is fifty-five dollars.'

'Right. I'll take the medium-sized one.'

After opting for the still overpriced 35-dollar flag, I noticed that it had been imported from Par near St Austell. To put this in context, I was paying about twenty pounds for a piece of cloth I could have bought for ten just down the road from my home. As I handed over the cash, Bateman entered the shop and joined us.

'Oh, and is this your friend?' asked Catherine.

'Yes. He's the reason I'm buying it, really,' I replied.

'Take a few postcards if you want,' she said, pointing at a revolving rack on the counter. 'And you must be missing tea. Have these tea bags.'

Catherine's generosity was like nothing I had ever experienced before. Not only had she opened the shop especially for us on her day off, but now she was searching round her counter for extras to add to my flag purchase.

'Oh, take more postcards than that. Have three or four,' she demanded, thrusting extra cards into a brown paper bag she had produced to place the goodies in. 'Oh, how rude of me. Have these Jaffa Cakes too.'

*

Bateman and I had planned on leaving Mineral Point after a quick browse around, but the warm welcome we had been given plus the people we had met (but minus the pasty we had eaten) added up to an impression of belonging, and although we were thousands of miles from home we felt an affectionate sense of family and kinship. It was now getting on for four o'clock and we decided it was too late to make our way to Chicago. Instead, we drove to Pendarvis for the final tour of the day.

Bateman and I along with eight other people waited patiently for the tour to begin. In the room in which we were asked to wait were maps and pictures of Cornwall and a portrait of Robert Neal, the man who preserved the Pendarvis cottages at a time when other stone dwellings were being torn down for their materials in the 1930s. As people checked their watches with increasing anxiety, I studied the other members of the group, wondering which one of them would be our guide. In the corner was an elderly couple who hadn't spoken since we walked in, not even to each other (maybe saving their breath to conduct a tour) and in front of them stood a small man with glasses who appeared to be unaccompanied and ready to round up his prospective clients. Outside stood a woman in an early 1900s gown and bonnet who wouldn't look out of place sitting in a rocking chair on the front of her porch, defending her ranch with a shotgun. Out of the possible candidates,

I must admit she appeared to be the favourite.

The tour was of the preserved cottages and their surroundings and concentrated on the early miners rather than the mine itself. As we were led through the small, granite houses and talked through the settlers' lives, our guide, who had turned out to be the woman in the bonnet, insisted on clarifying every fact with me, as if my Cornish upbringing had put me in a similar position to some kind of Ofsted inspector.

'They first made pies with fish in, didn't they?'

'I don't know. I had a pasty today, though, and it wasn't great. Does that help?'

It was relentlessly hot, and when the tour finally ended where all tours do – in the gift shop – a huge sense of relief was felt by everyone, none more so than me. I had to get back to the car; I'd left the Jaffa Cakes in there.

We returned to the Chamber of Commerce one final time and bade farewell to Joy, thanking her for her help and generosity. As a parting gift, she presented us with a Mineral Point T-shirt each and wished us luck for the remainder of our trip.

The following day we were due to arrive in Chicago, but although we were now more than halfway through the trip distance-wise, the spree was far from over. Mineral Point had been a welcome respite from law-breaking but I had never lost sight of my real reason for being in the US. I hadn't had much success on the West Coast or in the Midwest, but I was feeling pretty confident about the remainder of the trip. Eastern America contained more people, more towns and – more important – more bizarre laws. I left Mineral Point in an upbeat mood, not forgetting, before joining the road bound for Chicago, to make an essential purchase. I would need a pair of pyjamas for the law awaiting me in the Windy City.

10

The Reel Deal

Chicago, America's third largest city, was certainly a wake-up call. We hadn't stayed in a big metropolitan area since Salt Lake City and had certainly not experienced a city on quite the same scale since leaving Los Angeles. On the day of our arrival, the Windy City was very much overcast and breathless. Visibility was down to a couple of miles or so and the haze had descended onto the downtown area, smothering the skyscrapers and softening the otherwise dominating presence of the Sears Tower.

Any normal tourist heading towards the centre of the city might have wanted to visit Chicago's Chinatown district, tour the John Hancock Center or take a tour on Lake Michigan and study the city's stupendous architecture. Under normal circumstances, I would have joined them, but I had a completely different sort of itinerary planned for my stay here and headed towards the north of the city and Montrose Harbor, a destination which would probably not appear on a great many tourists' 'to do' lists.

Bizarrely, yet wonderfully, it is illegal in Chicago to fish in one's pyjamas. Apparently it's also illegal to catch a fish sitting on a giraffe's neck (the angler, not the fish). With pyjamas much more readily available than giraffes in department stores nowadays, I opted for the easier of the two.

As we approached Chicago, the suburbs of leafy neighbourhood streets and shopping precincts suddenly yielded to miles of industry. Where the view was once of houses, gardens and the occasional park, it was now an ugly spectacle of cargo containers, railway lines and dilapidated factory buildings – a sight in no way improved by the smoglike conditions of the day. Further into the city and approaching the downtown area, we crossed the Chicago River, passing the city's amphitheatric Soldier Field, a stadium with a capacity of almost 70,000 and home to the Chicago Bears football team. Entering Chicago's downtown area was a strangely humbling experience. To our right lay hundreds of stationary yachts bobbing docilely on the unruffled waters of Lake Michigan and to our left stood the intimidating view of corporate America – hundreds of concrete structures which had sprouted from the financially fertile land of the shore. Turning away again and back to the lake the complexion changed once more. The endless harbours and rows of yachts and other sailing vessels had suddenly parted, to be replaced by Navy Pier, which projected deep into Lake Michigan and featured a Ferris wheel, restaurants and bars in an evocative reminder of the British seaside. Finally, to my surprise, a beach appeared.

Even though I was born and brought up near the coast, this seemed surreal. Never in my life have I been so close to both people lazing on pristine white sands and the hustle of a busy metropolis. In Chicago, the two are only separated by six lanes of gridlocked traffic. My home is just as picturesque as the beaches on Chicago's coastline, but the nearest road with more than four lanes of traffic is over ninety miles away.

First impressions of Montrose Harbor were curious to say the least. After parking the car and taking a look around, I noticed there were no boats, no yachts and, rather crucially, no water. I referred to the map to see if we had arrived in the right place and discovered that the harbour was situated at the end of Lincoln Park. Judging by the dozens of soccer pitches I could see over the flapping pages of the map, Lincoln Park is where we must have been.

When we finally reached it, Montrose Harbor's amenities appeared to be numerous, with beaches, piers and hundreds of boats, and my first thought was that the Windy City's law was going to be a breeze. Fishing opportunities were plentiful and all I needed to do was find a quayside business which hired out rods. On the other side of the harbour and a good walk back in the direction of the car, another beach was hidden behind a concrete structure containing changing rooms for the beach patrons and an impressive archway leading to the beautiful shoreline. We stepped through the arch onto the beach's modest promenade, which was lightly covered in sand, and looked around for a hire centre. To my left were half a dozen children, each clutching an ice cream or a soft drink, and to my right stood what I was looking for. Phew. The rental sign informed me that from this hole-in-the-wall I could hire anything from a jet ski to a banana boat, but on closer inspection the relief was short-lived. I could hire a kayak, a surfboard, a wetsuit and maybe a rod if the business had not been boarded up and closed down indefinitely.

Making our way back to the harbour, and contemplating a drive into town to buy our props, I suddenly had an idea.

'I don't have to hire a rod, or even buy one,' I said to Bateman, who seemed to be growing ever more impatient. It was probably already beer o'clock for him. 'I'll just borrow one. All I have to do is find someone who'll let me.'

The harbour side was enormous and as we walked round the perimeter I felt sure we would find a fisherman who would be only too pleased to assist us. Fifteen minutes and one long walk later we had passed dozens of Americans who seemed kind and pleasant enough to fit the bill. Trouble was, they weren't fishing, and the only man who was sat cross-legged staring into the water and dropping and lifting a piece of string like a yo-yo. Bateman slyly pointed to him and suggested I should ask if I could hold his string after putting on my pyjamas.

'Hm. He's my number one reserve if I can't find anyone else, mate.'

We had almost reached the end of the harbour, passing such yachts as *Cat's Meow* and *No Inheritance*, when I spotted a bank leading to what must have been the lake. It was there, standing at the top of the incline, that I discovered where all the fishermen had been hiding from me. From the top, several concrete steps led to a flat twenty-foot breakwater where numerous fishermen sat waiting patiently with rods and cool boxes by their sides. One man and his son were fishing just at the foot of the steps where I stood. These were to be our targets, partly due to their friendly faces but mostly because they were closest and my feet were sore. Bateman and I sat on the bottom step and wondered how best to ask. Stuff it. There wasn't going to be an easy way, was there? Leaving my pyjamas in my rucksack, I made my way over to the father, thinking of my approach to Arden and formulating a similar style.

'Excuse me.' Good start. 'I have a rather bizarre request. I'm going round America breaking strange laws and it's illegal in Chicago to fish in your pyjamas. Now I have some pyjamas in my bag and all I'm really asking you is if I can hold your rod. I don't need to catch anything, just be seen to be fishing. Is that all right?'

The man laughed and scratched his head. 'Well, you're right about bizarre. But sure.' His son looked on, horrified, obviously wondering why his dad had answered the madman at all.

'All right, mate?' I asked him.

'Fine, thanks.' He turned his attention back to the water, his eyes widening.

I walked back to my rucksack and began to change into my nightwear. 'Wait until you see my pyjamas. These are great.'

The pyjamas, which were a few sizes too big for me, were the traditional collared, button-up kind and were grey with a navy-blue motif similar to badly drawn snowflakes. My new friends, Bill Stover and ten-year-old David, looked a little concerned now they had actually seen I wasn't winding them up and had the attire to prove it.

'Right, I'm ready.'

Bill had already reeled in his line and must have wanted me to do this thing properly.

'You know how to cast off, don't you?' he asked, pointing at the reel.

'I think so. Hold on to the line and flick this thingamajig,' I replied, showing off my knowledge of fishing terminology.

'That's right.'

After a simple but effective cast, the law had been broken. I didn't have to catch anything; I simply had to fish using a rod with bait on the line, and that I had achieved. David, who by now was standing a good twenty feet away from me, simply stood gazing out to sea, taking no notice of what I was doing. Maybe it wasn't the first time this had happened to him. I reeled the line back in and handed the rod back to his dad.

'Thanks, Bill. You've been a great help.'

'Where are you off to next then on this adventure?' he asked.

'Well, we're here for a couple more days and then we're heading for Indianapolis.'

'You do this by public transport?'

'No, hire car. It would be very difficult in this country to travel by public trans—' I looked down at what I was wearing. 'Hey, Bill. Maybe I should get changed before I begin a discussion about the inadequacy of America's public transportation. You mind?'

I returned to my bag, changed, and shook Bill's hand for a second time. He was clearly a soulmate. 'Hey,' he said. 'I'm not sure if it's illegal, but I cross-country skied across the Buckingham Fountain once when I was younger.'

'Really? We passed that. It's quite impressive. I'm pretty sure it would be illegal.'

As I shook David's hand and promised I would now leave them alone, I noticed he was wearing a Chicago Cubs T-shirt.

'You a Cubs fan then?' I asked him, in a last-ditch attempt to prove I wasn't a simple-minded idiot.

'Yeah.'

'We might go and see them in the next couple of days.'

'You can't. They're playing in Seattle.'

'Oh, right.' So much for my proof.

So the Cubs weren't playing at home in the next few days. I knew that Chicago had two baseball teams and that the Chicago White Sox were definitely in town and playing that afternoon. Thanking Bill and David one final time, we headed for the White Sox's stadium. America's national sport, no law-breaking and an afternoon outing suitable for the family was planned. What harm could possibly come to us?

U.S. Cellular Field, located a few miles south of the downtown area, is the home of the Chicago White Sox. The excitement of fishing had tired me out and I simply wanted to sit down amongst thousands of fans, watch baseball and try to learn the rules of the game. I should have plenty of time to get my head round the sport – the nine innings of play usually takes three hours to complete.

Two thirty on a Thursday afternoon seemed a rather strange time to me to stage a baseball game, but by the looks of the full-to-capacity parking lots and queues of people in White Sox shirts lining up behind the many ticket windows, it seemed that only the fans of the Chicago Cubs were at work today. It's probably because of the length of the games that not one of the hundreds of fans who found themselves still outside seemed at all concerned that the game against the Toronto Blue Jays had begun thirty minutes before they arrived. We joined the back of the shortest line and waited to reserve a seat in the crowd for the following day's evening game. The ubiquitous ticket touts surrounded the windows and unsuccessfully offered their tickets to passers-by and anyone who was already waiting patiently in line. Their salesmen skills were useless against my stonewall-like defence.

'I've got two tickets for upper reserved or bleachers. You want?'

'No thanks, mate. I don't have a clue what you're talking about.'

When we finally reached the front of the queue and enquired how much a ticket to the evening game the following day would be, we were informed that the only seats they had left to sell were upper tier seats with obscured view – affectionately referred to by all American sports fans as 'nose bleeders'. Ultimately, the humid temperature put Bateman and me off watching the afternoon game and we settled for returning to the car and watching a game in New York or Boston later in the holiday.

Leaving the ballpark and travelling east along city streets back to our motel, we seemed to have entered one of the roughest parts of the city. The sidewalks were littered and every convenience store had put up wrought-iron bars to protect their windows. As I drove through the ramshackle streets, trying not to make eye contact with anyone for fear of a gangland attack, a car coming from the opposite direction attempted to turn left across my path as I approached.

'What was he doing?' shouted Bateman. 'It was our right of way.'

There was only one thing missing from this scenario and it wasn't long before we heard it. A police siren echoed out loud and clear, or deafening and irritating, you could also say. I was waiting at a junction at the time and looked left and right in order to allow the police, wherever they were, to continue in their pursuit quickly and efficiently.

'Where's that coming from?' I asked Bateman. 'It's not anywhere down there.'

'It's not behind us, there's just a normal car there,' he replied.

We continued for a couple more blocks and heard the siren for a second time. Once again, the cops were nowhere to be seen, and we assumed they had turned off towards the scene of the crime. On we went. By now we must have driven half a mile or so after hearing the siren for the first time, and we grew concerned when the same noise was heard yet again. This time, however, the alarm was much more intense and sounded closer. Looking to my left, I noticed that the blue car that had been behind us had spontaneously accelerated and was now positioned alongside. The man travelling in the passenger seat demanded I pull over and, without thinking, I stopped the car and turned the engine off. The only thought I had was that it was a gangster's car. Perhaps they used the siren to pose as undercover policemen before they robbed you and took your vehicle. I was prepared to quickly drive away again, but the seconds I had wasted had given the three men in the car enough time to jump out and run to the front doors of the Chrysler. They were wearing bullet-proof vests, but I hadn't decided whether this was a good or a bad sign when Bateman, who had probably not thought of a gangland explanation for our halt, suddenly opened his door to see what the problem was. This was a big mistake.

'Show me your hands! Show me your hands!' demanded the man on his side, who by now had one hand resting on the gun in his holster. Bateman had no choice but to agree and slowly showed an empty right hand and a Chicago sightseeing guide in his left. I was having my own problems – I had two on my side.

'Open your window! Open your window!'

With utter confusion running through my head I couldn't think how to operate the car window.

'Do it now!' screamed the cop.

I quickly remembered the windows were electric and after turning the ignition key – simultaneously miming that I wasn't going to drive away – managed successfully to comply with the demand. I made sure to remain in my seat and made no sudden movements, especially not to open my door. The cop stood sternly.

'Were you ever planning on stopping at those stop signs?'

Time to play ignorant. 'Stop signs, officer? I didn't

see any. Did you, Bateman?' Bateman shook his head.

'Well, you run two of them back there. Almost causing an accident at the first.' I didn't want to point out that surely whatever 'running a stop sign' was it should have been 'ran'.

'Did I? Well, I'm terribly sorry. I'm from England and still getting used to the roads here.'

The mention of England seemed to relax the cop and his whole posture and pattern of speech loosened. He turned to his colleague behind him, smiled and gestured towards us. 'They're from England.'

Cop number three, who hadn't spoken a word up to this point, and was bizarrely sporting a marijuana medallion, had heard where we were from and, obviously wanting to jokingly insult us, leaned in front of his partner and up to my window. 'G'day!'

Maybe he should stick to being the quiet, daunting type.

My ignorance and nationality apparently proved my innocence, but the cop looked in through my windows and had a final question for me after seeing the pyjamas resting on the back seat.

'What's that flag in the back?' he asked.

'It's a Cornish flag.'

'Cornish? What's that?'

'We're from a part of England called Cornwall and that's its flag.'

'Cornwall?'

I decided not to lecture a man with a gun. 'It's an English flag, OK?'

'Oh, an English flag. I get ya. Cos you're from England, right? Anyway, where you headed?'

'Trying to get back to the interstate.'

'It's straight up and then make a left.'

With that taken care of, the cops seemed to have forgotten all about any offence I may have committed earlier. Obviously, driving through a few stop signs was a far more serious crime than fishing in your pyjamas.

That night in the Kerry Piper Irish Bar just yards from our motel the quiz night was well under way when Bateman and I sat at the only two empty chairs we could find – at one of the four bench-like tables which created a square round the pub's central wooden pillar. Sitting across from us was a team with only two members, and they didn't appear to be doing too well. Joey and his partner Jackie were both music teachers and worked at a middle school just south of Chicago. After chatting with them for some time, when the second half of the quiz began I gave them a bit of a hand if I had an inkling of what the answer might have been, shaking my head and shrugging my shoulders whenever an American sport was mentioned. It was clear from the confident look of the other teams and the fact that our combined specialist subjects of music and bizarre American laws were probably not a formula for victory that we were a newly formed team which was destined for failure.

'How was Edward Teach better known?'

'I reckon it's Blackbeard the pirate. I think I've heard it somewhere. What have you put down?' I asked Joey encouragingly.

'Edward Scissorhands,' Jackie replied. Yep, I was right about our chances.

When the results of the quiz were revealed, it was clear that, other than the Edward Teach question, the only thing I had got completely and categorically correct was that we were, indeed, always destined for defeat.

It was nearing closing time, and as Bateman joined Joey and Jackie at the piano on stage I got chatting to the quizmaster and members of the team who sat behind us and had beaten us quite convincingly. When I revealed the nature of my trip, Ann Traczek and the other members of her team seemed overjoyed with the whole idea.

'Well there're plenty of them,' she remarked. 'It sounds like fun. Where are you going next?'

I realized Ann was a remarkably intelligent woman when she revealed her love for English soccer and Manchester United, and her husband's support of Arsenal, while the rest of her team were Liverpool fans. I instantly liked her when she immediately corrected herself. 'Sorry, around you I should say foot-ball.'

We talked until we were asked to leave, and before we parted company I told Ann what had happened to us that afternoon and how I couldn't get my head round the fact that the mood of the ordeal we had been subjected to had changed so dramatically. It had begun and ended on two completely different notes: beginning almost at gunpoint and ending just minutes later with a discussion about flags and a very helpful direction leading us back to our motel. Ann nodded understandingly but was not at all surprised at what had happened. Our Cornish flag, a white cross on a black background, was similar to the emblem of the Black Gangster Disciples, one of the biggest and most violent gangs in Chicago.

11

Coming to You Live

Although it wasn't an absolute necessity to wake up at stupid o'clock in the morning, on the day on which we were going to change our car and drive to Indianapolis, my wake-up call was provided for me by BBC Radio Cornwall.

I had promised to keep in touch with many of the local and national radio stations to report my progress in America, but with the time difference making early morning interviews a menace I opted to stay loyal to my local BBC radio station and agreed to do an interview with David White of Radio Cornwall. Shortly before six in the morning, my hotel room's phone rang and before I realized what country I was in the receiver was next to my ear and I was talking live to David and his discerning listeners.

'Hi, Rich. How're things going? How many laws are

you up to?' he asked ebulliently after apologizing for the absurdity of the time at which he was calling.

'Well, it's not even six o'clock here, Dave, so you must bear with me.'

After describing my pyjama success of the previous day, I explained – poorly – about the spot of bother running a stop sign had caused us. So much so that, two minutes in, even I didn't know what I was talking about.

'Well, you seem to be having fun. How's your friend?' he asked, saving me the embarrassment of digging myself into a deeper hole.

'Funny you should ask, actually. His name is Luke Bateman and apparently your parents used to baby-sit him. Are your parents called Anne and Alex?'

'Oh yeah, I know him.'

Luckily, the fact that David had me on at the very end of his show to make the time difference easier for me meant that Cornwall needed to hear the region's news shortly after that and I could pull the sheet back over my head and return to my slumber.

Leaving Chicago wasn't as straightforward as normal. Usually, we would consult the map and make our way in whatever direction the next law took us, but before we left the Windy City we had to change our hire car as the three-week lease had expired. The car company had not allowed us to take the same car for as long as we needed and to a destination as far away as New York, and so we had to change over in Chicago if we wanted to continue driving to the Big Apple.

Luckily, the rental company's base in Chicago was at Midway International Airport and not the city's monolithic O'Hare International which is Chicago's, America's and the world's busiest airport. No party or celebration greeted us on the completion of the first leg of our journey, just a simple low-key 'Park it there' as we pulled into the second floor of a multi-storey car park which acted as the pick-up and drop-off point for our and three other rental companies. As Bateman enquired where we would have to go to sign the paperwork and pay for our next car, I took a look around the vehicles available for hire and, remembering the words of Brenda the psychic, was hoping for a very small number of red ones. Bateman returned and must have noticed my peculiar behaviour as I peered around concrete pillars for better views.

'What are you doing?'

'Nothing much. Just looking at what we might get.'

'You're looking for a red one, aren't you? You really believed that woman.'

'No, I'm just seeing if there are any good ones, that's all.'

'I've already looked. That Jeep appears to be the only red vehicle here, anyway,' he said, pointing at a Jeep Wrangler parked in the corner.

Phew.

After getting lost in a stairwell and finally taking the lift, we found ourselves in Baggage Collection where the rental companies' representatives were. We were greeted by a delightfully pleasant young woman.

'Hi! How can I help you?'

'Good afternoon. We've just dropped off our car and we're here to pick up another. It's reserved under the name Smith.'

The desk clerk looked away and glanced at her screen for a few seconds, typing occasionally. 'And you're taking the car to New York City?'

'Yes.'

'And you do know there's a drop-off charge for that?'

'Yep.'

She stared at the screen once again. 'And your quoted price was...' She gasped. 'Oh, that is expensive, isn't it?'

'Yeah. It's because we're not twenty-five.'

'Well, I can give you a free upgrade if you want?'

This was great news. The car we had reserved was probably the smallest kind they had and Bateman had already threatened to refuse it if it turned out to be similar in size to a Ford Fiesta or Mini Metro.

'I can offer you a Jeep?'

Bateman smiled and leaned forward. 'A Jeep? It doesn't happen to be red, does it?'

The lady glanced back at her screen, pressed a few keys and smiled. 'It does, actually. How did you know that?'

'Just a hunch.'

Bateman turned and stared at me, leaning on the counter. 'Shall we get the *red* Jeep then?' he asked smugly. I guessed there was nothing wrong with accepting the Jeep. It was certainly red but how would I look if I took the words of some crackpot seriously? A Jeep isn't even a car and it wasn't as if hiring the thing meant that I was being offered a lift in it, was it? Was it?

'OK, let's take it,' I said decisively.

'Although a Jeep isn't the best form of vehicle to do another five thousand miles in, is it?' replied Bateman.

'No, course not. Let's not take it.'

I'd had a lucky escape. I wasn't scared anyway; of course I wasn't. I was fully prepared to accept the Jeep until Bateman expressed doubts about the comfort of the vehicle for such a long journey. The psychic was probably lying, just as I thought when I had originally met her. I turned to the clerk to show my nonchalant and unruffled machismo.

'I've upgraded you to a Dodge Neon,' she remarked as she tore the receipt out of the printer.

'What colour's that?'

Our Dodge Neon, a shade of turquoise or royal blue and definitely without any hint of red, already had miles on the clock and certainly didn't compare to the Sebring. Its beige interior was unimpressive and the passenger seat's stains made us feel as if we had borrowed the car from a friend. A not particularly hygienic friend. As we pulled away from the airport and onto the freeway, the car's main attributes appeared similar to the first's: when the accelerator pedal was firmly pushed to the floor, the car would respond by making as much noise as possible without actually increasing in speed. Bateman wasn't as annoyed as I would have thought he would be and the reason soon became apparent – this car had a cigarette lighter.

Indianapolis is a clean, neat and unobtrusive city. Its uncluttered streets and roads make a refreshing change from other American cities. But then again, Indianapolis is less than two hundred years old.

When Indiana became the nineteenth state in 1816, its capital was a small town called Corydon. By 1825, the state was looking for another town to be its permanent capital and, only four years after it had been laid out, Indianapolis was selected. It was clear that the city had been planned with the specific intention of housing government buildings. Although the city's downtown area was similar to that of any other American metropolis, with high-rise buildings towering above well-known high-street outlets and fast-food retailers, its central business district seemed to have been scaled down. Our motel, on its own in a flat area surrounded by disused car parks, stood by a road leading between the skyscrapers to the Monument Circle roundabout in the heart of the city.

The Soldiers and Sailors Monument stands as the centrepiece of Monument Circle and, with its towering obelisk, artistic sculpture and fountains, is as impressive a structure as any I've seen in Europe. It would also most definitely appear if a series entitled

America's Greatest Roundabouts was ever made (watch this space).

The 230-foot tower was dedicated in 1902 to all of Indiana's heroes who had died in battles up to that date, and after circling the tower once I was surprised at how often Indiana was called into action. Soldiers lost in the 1861–65 War for the Union, 1846–48 War with Mexico, the Indian and British Wars of 1812, and the War of the Revolution and the capture of Vincennes from the British in 1779 featured on the four sides of the monument. I wasn't here for a history lesson, however, and the only reason I was standing in the centre of the city was to locate the Emmis Communications Building which stood at 40 Monument Circle. The cause of my being in Indianapolis at all was a promise I had made to the two hosts of a breakfast show in the city. Basically, I had travelled two hundred miles out of my way simply because I wanted to meet a man whose name was Wank.

When I first spoke to Ed Wank and his co-host Dave O'Brien back in March, I had promised that I would keep in touch with them as my trip progressed and now, because I was in the city and still found his name childishly amusing, I was going to appear on their breakfast show the following day. Now I knew where the building was, I didn't have to wake up so early.

Thinking Ed and Dave would probably ask what laws pertained to Indiana and particularly its capital,

I rummaged through my bag and found my book of laws. In South Bend it is illegal for a monkey to smoke cigarettes; reading on, I discovered that an ape actually stood trial, was found guilty and ordered to pay a 25-dollar fine as well as the cost of the trial. Pi, known throughout the world as 3.1415926535897932384626433832795028841972 (to 40 decimal places), in Indiana is simply known as 4. This makes calculating circumference and area of circles a lot easier throughout the state, but surely the way to produce marginally more accurate results would be to round it down to 3. Just for the radio show the following day, I found a law that was relevant to the entire state and one I could easily break that evening.

'Let's go to the cinema, Bateman.'

'Why? What's on?'

'I dunno. But it's illegal to ride on a streetcar or enter a cinema or theatre within three hours of eating garlic. I'm going to break the law, seeing as we're here. Do you know where I can get some garlic from? I'm gonna eat a whole one.'

'You're going to eat an entire garlic? You'll die,' Bateman warned. 'Just one clove is bad enough.'

'I'm not even sure if I like garlic, actually.'

I picked up the phone and asked for a pizza to be delivered to our room, making sure to ask for lots of garlic bread. Bateman looked on.

'You ain't sitting anywhere near me in the cinema.'

I managed to eat two rather large pieces of garlic

bread along with a chicken-topped pizza before we made our way to the cinema complex, located in the mall a couple of blocks from Monument Circle. The cinema was a multi-screen and the list of movies showing was immense. Unfortunately, they all seemed a bit dull and there was nothing I was particularly keen to see. In the end, Bateman and I found ourselves in a 470-seat cinema with only nine other people watching *The Dukes of Hazzard*.

I was glad when the film was over. My memories of a perfectly good eighties TV series were now tarnished beyond repair. Not even the legs of Jessica Simpson as Daisy Duke could save a movie which stank as badly as my breath. Bateman, who had any of the other 460 seats to choose from, had plonked himself in a seat just four from my own, and seemed to enjoy the movie but probably not the company.

'I can still bloody smell you from here!'

At seven o'clock the following morning my alarm clock woke me. Stepping into the shower, I realized it was the earliest I had got out of bed on the entire holiday. Later, when we left for the radio station, I noticed that the gravel-laden car park opposite our motel had been the venue for Elvis Presley's last ever concert.

Back in March, the Wank and O'Brien breakfast show had been on what was then known as Real 97.1. Between now and then, the show had shifted dramatically from an adult contemporary station to a broadcaster of country and western called Hank FM. Nearly every radio and local television station in America is represented by a not very memorable four-letter combination and the companies that broadcast from the Emmis Communications Building were no exception. This building housed WYXB, WNOU, WIBC and Hank FM's pseudonym WLHK. Thinking that whoever named the stations was probably the same idiot behind the lettering of the roads outside Mineral Point, I entered the building and was shown to the lift by the security guard. We were greeted by Angela, the intern on the breakfast show, who asked us to wait in the station's lounge and listen to the show in progress. The hosts were currently in the middle of an interview with a singer named Brad Cotter and sounded friendly and affable while conversing with their guest – rather than being intent on taking a pop at him – a quality now almost unheard of in radio. From what I could make out, Brad Cotter was the winner of the country and western version of *Pop Idol* (the unimaginatively named Nashville Star, not Pop Bridle which I thought would be rather more fitting) and had just released his debut single which he hoped would help raise money for the military families who had lost loved ones in Iraq and Afghanistan. Ed then introduced the single, 'An American Dream'.

Brad's voice, like all singers' of that ilk, was powerful and inspiring and reinforced the sentiment of the song. The gist of the lines which featured in every verse was a stirring mix of patriotism and national identity, with frequent mentions of stars, stripes and other symbolic reminders. The chorus, heartfelt and rousing, was aimed at evoking the raw emotions of every proud American and kindling their passion for the virtues of the flag. I'm sure people all round the Indianapolis area were pulling their cars over to the side of the road to release the tears they could no longer hold back, but I thought the song, despite being in aid of a very worthy cause, would be disliked in every country of the world but one. I don't know if any country is as defensive of its patriotism and its military as the US.

The spacious, minimalistic layout of the lounge made me feel as if Bateman and I were the first guests to arrive at a rather exclusive party. When Brad Cotter's interview had come to an end, I realized I was definitely not the guest of honour – that was clearly Mr Cotter who, as I had imagined he would be, was dressed in jeans, shirt and the obligatory cowboy hat. Along with his agent, press representatives and numerous other associates, he came through the lounge on his way out of the studio, and it was obvious that the man in the middle, guitar in hand, and surrounded by a flurry of attention, was the Nashville Star himself. As he passed our seats, he took the time to shake my hand and we were formally introduced by Angela.

'Heard your song, mate. It was really good,' I said.

I returned to my seat next to Bateman, relishing the

beauty of sarcasm and the Americans' failure to ever detect a single hint of it. We watched the singer formally shake hands with the station's representatives before being scuttled into the lift to continue his hectic schedule. I must admit, I felt a tad jealous of the attention he was getting, but I supposed it was justified. He would soon be an international recording artist; he had places to be, people to meet and videos to shoot. I was simply here to meet a guy with a funny name and I probably still reeked of garlic.

The Wank and O'Brien Show was broadcast from a room on the sixth floor of the building with a view of the impressive roundabout. From their huge studio window, I could see that Monument Square was still perfectly serene although rush hour was fast approaching. I took my seat in between what I could only assume were the producer and the telephonist who also worked on the show. Ed Wank, his bald head reflecting the studio lights, sat furthest away from me on the opposite end of the rounded table, and sported a white T-shirt, jeans and distinctive thick-framed glasses. Dave O'Brien, with whom I had exchanged emails, was the first of the two to greet me.

'Hiya, Richard. Thanks for coming. How are you finding Indianapolis?'

'Yeah, OK. Very clean, very nice. Purpose built. Nice roundabout,' I rambled.

Dave looked as if he had always been a cowboy and seemed to fit into the country and western broadcaster mould very comfortably. He was even taller than me at about six foot six, with dark greying hair, and wore jeans, a loose, casual shirt and a very country and western goatee beard with connecting moustache. I thought of Brad Cotter, Hank FM (with five banners and boards dotted around the studio bearing the name I could hardly forget it) and how very un-country and western I must appear. Apart from riding a horse once when I was ten and being subjected to the many John Denver singles in my dad's record collection, I was hardly in the same league.

Over a Shania Twain hit and the obligatory advertisement break, Dave made idle small talk about my journey so far to put me at my ease, while Ed used any gap on air available to him to promote their next guest.

'We have a real criminal in the studio with us and he'll be coming up next.'

When the time came, I was totally relaxed and enjoyed every minute in the limelight. I completely ignored their opening question of 'How are you, Rich?' and went straight for the jugular.

'Your real name is Wank?' I asked. 'You should have gone to a high school in England. You would have had the mickey really taken out of you with a surname like that!'

The interview must have lasted for about ten minutes (twenty with adverts and songs). After my admission that I had eaten garlic within three hours of going to the cinema the previous evening in honour of being invited to their city, we ended on a bizarre note about Americans' outrage at being made to pay over two dollars for a gallon of petrol. I subjected them to equal measures of shock and relief when I revealed that, even with the favourable exchange rate, the British pay over six dollars a gallon.

'Thanks for popping in, Rich,' said Dave, beginning to fade in yet another hit.

'It's been a pleasure.'

'And people can follow your progress on your website or something?' he added as the song's intro-duction raced towards the opening lyrics.

I knew how radio worked. I had to get a last line in before the lyrics.

'They can follow our progress if they want but they'd have to do it in their own car!'

Although I hadn't expected to, I very much enjoyed our stopover in Indianapolis. It may not be the biggest or most exciting city in America, and with a nickname like 'America's Crossroads' it was hardly the most picturesque either. But what was well hidden in the avenues and streets of the city was something I can now use as a measuring stick to judge how friendly and helpful the residents of a particular city are. Indianapolis's tramps are the friendliest and most courteous I've ever met. If the poorest, most down-trodden vagrants of a city are jolly and upbeat, then surely that speaks volumes for the overall mood.

I wasn't 100 per cent sure that the woman who appeared behind us as we waited to cross the road was a tramp as she made no attempt to ask for any money, but since she had no shoes on her feet and her only possession seemed to be a small plastic bag which hung loosely from her right wrist, I guessed that she was.

'Whoa! Jesus!' she shouted as she peered into a large metal grid covering whatever lay beneath the sidewalk before moving on to the next grid, bending over as before and staring into the drop. 'Whoa! Jesus!'

Indianapolis was fast becoming my favourite metropolis and although by world standards the city had no history or culture whatsoever, it was a complete joy to simply amble the streets. It wasn't long before we were approached by a homeless man who was in charge of sports development and taught me some basketball moves in exchange for a few cents, and then another vagrant pointed us back in the direction of our motel. We weren't lost and I knew exactly where the motel was but it was a kind gesture born of the city's overwhelming and unquestionable benevolence. As we thanked the gentleman and went on our way, he called us back and showed us a handful of identical pictures of the city's capitol building which had somehow come into his possession.

'Here, boys; have a postcard.'

12

Blues Booze

We arrived in St Louis, four hours from Indianapolis, in the late afternoon and Bateman seemed to have just one thing in mind.

'Let's go to Hooters!'

'I'm not really that hungry right now, mate.'

'Nor am I. I just wanna go to Hooters.'

How could I refuse? I didn't want to disappoint Bateman and if I had to keep him happy by visiting a restaurant where girls wearing small orange shorts and skin-hugging vests brought pitchers of lager to your table, I was willing to make the sacrifice. Over a couple of beers, we began to discuss the reason for our being in St Louis.

'So, what law is it today then?'

'It's illegal here to drink beer out of a bucket whilst sitting on a street kerb. Don't know why.'

'OK,' replied Bateman, who seemed to be at ease with the entire absurdity of it all.

St Louis, it appeared, wasn't the only place to have such an odd decree. I could have broken this one in the Pullman area of Chicago if I had not been busy fishing in my pyjamas or evading cops in the world's slowest ever car chase. My brand-new bucket had cost me $1.04 (Missouri had lower sales tax rates at 4.225) in another local dollar shop. I rejoined Bateman in the car with a spring in my step and a bucket containing a single can of lager in my hand. I was ready.

St Louis, home of blues and jazz music, and the birthplace of both T. S. Eliot and Chuck Berry, was founded by French fur trader Pierre Laclède in 1764. Since that time, the city has been under both French and Spanish rule and the mass immigration which St Louis experienced when the Americans bought the state from the French seems to have disguised any visible links to its colonial past. And it would not even come close to competing on the same level as Indianapolis in the tramp stakes.

The road we selected to take us to the heart of the city must have passed through the roughest and poorest parts of St Louis. When we stopped at a petrol station to buy fuel, Bateman went to pay and on his way back to the car was approached by a woman who asked for some money. Normally, in any such trans-action, a collection of small change is gratefully received and you are thanked for your consideration and leave with a sense of compassion. Things obviously worked slightly differently in St Louis. This woman didn't even seem pleased when Bateman finally succumbed to her nagging and proffered two dollars. He was seething when he got back in the car.

'I gave her a couple of bucks and she asked for more! Cheeky bitch.'

We parked by the riverfront where the Mississippi River separates St Louis, Missouri from East St Louis in Illinois, and were confronted with the defining symbol of St Louis ... and another tramp. The 630-foot Gateway Arch is the largest structure in the city and is basically a large piece of curved metal that couldn't look more out of place if it tried. Nevertheless, standing beneath the construction, in between the two stainless steel bases, and staring up at its peak, you can only marvel at such a superb piece of engineering. It is strangely beautiful, visually phenomenal and absolutely pointless – and cost fifteen million dollars back in 1963. Only a city which had once passed a law forbidding the drinking of lager out of a bucket could commission an arc which was erected for the sole purpose of symbolizing the gateway to the American West.

We returned to the car and I grabbed the bucket and can of lager and made my way to a suitable sidewalk where a picture could be taken of me with the arch in the background. This was to prove I was in St Louis and that no cheap chicanery had taken place. As we strolled down the street back towards the arch, Bateman and I were stopped in the street by ... yep, you've guessed it; another beggar. The gentleman, in jeans and a white T-shirt, paid no attention to the strange mix of objects I had in my possession and began to plead his case.

'Look, man,' he began, 'my mama's dead.'

'I'm sorry to hear that,' I replied.

'Yeah. I haven't eaten in like a week,' he said, lifting his shirt to reveal a stomach which didn't look too undernourished to me. I wasn't sure he wasn't developing a six-pack. 'I was wondering if you had any money so I could get some food. You can't get anything in this city for under ten bucks.'

Ten dollars! He wanted ten dollars? This was a far cry from the Great British tramp, and St Louis was certainly leagues behind Indianapolis.

'I don't have ten dollars, mate, but you can have all the change I've got.' Wanting to get on with the law-breaking, I emptied my wallet and thrust what must have been more than a dollar into his hand. Bateman did the same. Unimpressed, the man turned and simply walked away without a word.

'He didn't even thank us,' Bateman yelled in disbelief.

'He didn't even give us a postcard, either.'

With no ungrateful tramps to disturb me, I sat down on the side of the kerb and opened the can of lager. My previous experience of working behind a bar was no help to me at all when it came to pouring lager into a bucket, so the result consisted mostly of head. Just as I raised the plastic pail to my mouth, a car pulled up and waited at the traffic lights beside me. Although the monolithic Gateway Arch stood directly in front of the passengers, their interest was firmly on me and what I was doing. For the briefest of moments, I was St Louis's newest and shortest-lived tourist attraction – the idiot sitting on a kerb drinking out of a bucket. After two mouthfuls I looked up at my audience and realized they weren't laughing, but seemed to be looking on with pity and concern. I probably should have asked for money to see if it worked as well for me as it did for everyone else I had met in the city, but the light had turned to green and their brief association with street crime was at an end. Our new tally was thirteen laws and victory had been achieved in eight of them. It was time for a celebration St Louis style.

I was told that before I left St Louis I should experience one of the many jazz bars that are synonymous with the city. As we ventured south to find a suitable venue, I thought it strange that in a city so famous for its music, the only things I noticed in the downtown area were banks, expensive hotels and tramps, none of which seemed jazzy in the slightest. I can't say I was imagining Louis Armstrong lookalike contests or saxophonists playing on street corners, but there was nothing at all which shouted out – or even whispered – to me that this was a town famous for the blues. At the southern end of Broadway we parked in a dark and gloomy area overshadowed by the freeway which ran above us. This part of Broadway, it seemed from the vast array of clubs, was the jazz capital of St Louis, and the only decision we had to make now was which one we should enter. Three or four similar clubs straddled the dark road and every single one appeared to have a live band. The first we passed turned out to be the most expensive and the empty seats and lack of audience kept us walking in search of a place which was bursting with energy. Then, like buses, two came along together. They both had live bands, which appeared to be mandatory, but there was an obvious winner. Although the club across the road had an outdoor seating area with colourful paper lanterns and rounded bulbs like the deck of a river party boat, it was, after all, across the road and a full sixty yards away, while the club we were standing directly outside was within falling distance and had two empty seats at the bar.

BB's Jazz, Blues and Soups, a nightspot which proudly boasts that the building has been used as a boarding house and as a 'house of ill repute', was jam-packed and it was completely understandable why the two vacant seats we had seen through the window had been occupied by other patrons by the time Bateman and I finally reached them. We stood back from the bar with the many other people who had arrived too late for a seat, and we blended in quite well. All walks of life jostled shoulders as people attempted to squeeze their way through the packed space in search of one of the small tables in the centre of the bar, each of which had its own table light. The glow of the red lampshades and the smoky atmosphere reminded me of the villain's gentlemen's club in a James Bond movie. From what I could make out, there were going to be a dozen acts throughout the evening, and each one therefore was only allowed a strictly limited time on stage. As we got the first round in, there was a changeover taking place and the MC welcomed Skeet Rodgers and the Inner City Blues Band (a name which was unforgettable thanks both to its length and to the fact that their adoring fans held a banner aloft throughout the thrilling performance). Skeet Rodgers was definitely on fire and the standing ovation the band received when they finished was proof. I agreed with the audience but directed the bulk of my applause to the row of ladies who had held the banner, whose arms must have been aching like mad. A remarkable act of fan fortitude.

As Skeet and his posse left the stage to make room for the next act, I looked around the room. Huddled on what I assumed was normally the dance floor were rows of tables where the real jazz and blues fans sat with friends and co-workers enjoying every minute of what was on show. The walls of the club were adorned with photo after photo of musical legends. BB King, Johnny Copeland and James Cotton hung along-side popular jazz artists such as Louis Armstrong and Billie Holiday in a who's who gallery of iconic figures. It wasn't until I placed my beer on a table further along the wall that I noticed a sign not dedicated to a jazz or blues star but aimed at me more than anyone else in the building. The sign simply read:

Sec. 14-03-070.

It is against city ordinances in any street, sidewalk, parking lot or alley to consume alcoholic beverages. This will result in a $500 fine or not more than 90 days in jail.

There was no mention of a bucket and it was obvious that the sign was just an official way of saying 'Don't take your drinks outside' to the clientele, but it was just a tad too coincidental for my liking.

The next day, it was time for our short stay in St Louis to come to an end. Neither of us was too upset. One of the most significant things about St Louis was that it made us reconsider whether we'd go to any more big cities soon. It was becoming clear that I genuinely enjoyed the smaller towns and meeting the people who lived there. Small-town America is fascinating, full of obscurities and intrigue. Getting to such places, or any other place, however, seemed to be a bit problematic.

'Why isn't the bloody boot opening?' Bateman shouted, frantically pressing the boot-lock button on the key.

'Has it run out of batteries?'

Whatever the reason, the boot refused to open and Bateman tried to unlock the doors instead.

'It doesn't even unlock it! What's going on?'

I took a step back and shrugged before I noticed the car's registration. I had learned the Sebring's number off by heart owing to the number of times I was asked to write it when checking into motels; this one I hadn't, but I was sure it was registered to the state of Michigan. This car wasn't. I approached Bateman and tapped him gently on the shoulder.

'Bateman, it's not our car. That's our one there.' I turned him round and pointed to an identical-looking vehicle. Well, it wasn't exactly identical; its boot was wide open.

Travelling south and crossing the Mississippi River for the third and final time, we entered the state of Tennessee. I hoped my brief encounter with a country and western star had me fully prepared for an aquatic version of a typical cowboy activity.

13

Jail Bait

If our first crossing of the Mississippi signified our arrival in eastern America en route to Chicago, our third, entering Tennessee, was an indicator that we had entered the Deep South. When we pulled off the interstate and into a rest area, I popped into the tourist information centre and looked round for a motel coupon guide as I usually do when entering a new state. The coupon guides, aimed at tourists travelling through the country, are great not only for finding accommodation whilst travelling on interstates but also for saving a few bucks. The information centre was empty and the clerk stood expectantly by her desk, ready to help me.

'Hi. I was just after one of these motel coupon things.'

I would tell you what her exact reply was but I

didn't understand a word she said. Her thick, impenetrable accent cemented the fact that we were very definitely in the south.

In the Tennessee Welcome Center in Memphis I did manage to understand what Precious in customer services was saying and with her help I was able to locate the closest state park where fishing was permitted. It seemed I was destined for the town of Millington, just north of Memphis, and the Meeman-Shelby State Park.

It is one of the most bizarre laws that I came across in my research. In the state of Tennessee it is illegal to catch a fish with a lasso. Actually, it's also illegal to catch a fish with your bare hands in Kansas, though I thought that might be raising the bar a little too high so Tennessee's obscure angling decree got the nod. I had already savoured the sweet taste of success in my previous two aquatic endeavours, spear hunting in Utah and fishing in my pyjamas in Chicago, so I was pretty confident. The only problem that concerned me was the wording. In Chicago I only had to fish and simply holding the rod was adequate, and in Utah all I had to do was hunt for a whale regardless of whether I found one or not. This was the first time where something had to be caught in order for the law to be broken. Success was not going to be guaranteed, and indeed was virtually impossible if I attempted to lasso the fish in the traditional way. It was time to visit the local hardware store for supplies.

Obviously rope was a necessity. A store employee

kindly showed me the way to the appropriate aisle but I was still, in effect, lost: the enormous selection on offer was incomprehensible and the feeling similar to visiting a Starbucks and being offered anything from an Arabian Mocha Sanani to a Colombian Narino Supremo when all you want is a cup of coffee. I did have a look for lasso rope to see if such a thing existed. It didn't. I settled for a twenty-foot length which probably had its own technical name but which I came to know as a pretty thick piece of white rope. Luckily, Millington had the ubiquitous Wal-Mart just down the road from the hardware store, and it was about to be called upon for a second time to supply the materials for a cheap but effective piece of fishing equipment.

The discovery of an Eagle Claw Catfish Outfit completed my search. The set included, among other fishing equipment, floats, weights and a selection of hooks. Off we went to the Meeman-Shelby State Park where law fourteen was to be tackled.

The road to the park took us through such towns as Cuba and Locke and, this being down south, the road appeared to be lined with more churches than houses. As it was a Wednesday, entrance to the park was free – not that it would have mattered. There was no toll-booth or barrier gate and instead the system of payment was simple and honesty-based. On any other day of the week you would pay the three-dollar tariff and take one of the park's rear mirror hangers which lay on top of the honesty box and could be taken for free anyway. Not that I would have even dreamed of doing such a thing – I'm not one to break the law.

The whole park seemed deserted and even when I arrived at the visitors' centre to pick up a map of the area there was little sign of staff, let alone visitors. The map showed that the biggest and most popular fishing spot was known as Poplar Tree Lake and had a pier, some sort of museum and a boat hire centre. It sounded ideal.

In reality Poplar Tree Lake wasn't the most idyllic of fishing hotspots. The pier turned out to be a small wooden jetty that protruded just twenty or so feet into the brown and murky-looking water of the lake, the museum was a display of stuffed wild animals, and the boat hire centre (a circular hut) was shut for lunch, and not due to reopen for another three-quarters of an hour. The lake itself was vast and deserted. If the state park was frequented at all at this time of year, the visitors didn't seem to come to Poplar, and our car was one of only three vehicles in the car park, one of which must have belonged to the woman on the pier who was the only person fishing.

Although the temperature was now back in the high thirties for the first time since Arizona, I was determined to make this law a fourth victory in a row – unprecedented! – and removed the materials from the boot of the car to construct my lasso.

It was obvious I was never going to catch a fish using the traditional lassoing technique of spin, throw, land and tighten – the fish might not have been clever enough to realize it but I knew from my research that even if I could throw the rope, it wouldn't penetrate the water. Not even a trained lasso artist could do that. My scheme was cleverer. Oh yes. Tying the end of the rope to itself and creating a lasso, I then tied catgut line to the noose and attached the hook. The bait supplied in the box kit was similar in appearance to an OXO cube and reeked of something unimaginable that only a fish would be stupid enough to taste. The lasso with line and hook was complete. If I were to catch a fish with my new creation, it would definitely have been caught with the lasso.

Still with thirty minutes remaining until we could hire a boat, it was decided that we would try our hand at fishing from the bank – preferably from under a nearby tree so we could shelter from the heat of the day. Within a minute of my maiden cast, the line was quickly tangled up in the roots by the shore and I managed to lose my hook, my bait and, with them, my dignity. God, this was going to be difficult. Why on earth was it a law anyway? I could fathom a guess as to why most of the others were in existence, but this one really flummoxed me. Anyone who did manage to catch a fish with a lasso should be held aloft, not held in custody. In a way, it would be similar to streaking at a sports event: you know what you've done is admirable and courageous and will be talked about for years but, at the end of it all, you're going to be arrested.

'I think we're going to have to hire a boat, mate,' I said, pulling my soggy line back out of the water.

At precisely one o'clock we waited outside the hire centre. Although the water seemed too dirty for any kind of life to survive in, the many pictures on display of fishermen holding outstanding bass and other varieties of fish from bream to catfish seemed to suggest I was wrong.

Ten minutes later another pick-up truck entered the car park and the driver made his way towards his hut. The gentleman, garbed in jeans and a brown T-shirt with the word 'Tennessee' emblazoned on the chest in case he forgot where he was, looked warily at me as if I was his first customer in a very long time. Judging from the hire book, I probably was.

'Hiya. I'd like to hire a boat for the afternoon, please.'

'Just the two of you, is it?'

'It is.'

'Can you sign here, please?'

As I signed the standard disclaimer which put all legal responsibility onto my shoulders in the event that I died, I noticed that a fishing permit was required. Although it was only three dollars, they were only available from the local shop, over five miles away down single-lane woodland roads. I wasn't prepared to waste precious time for that.

'You gonna go fishing?' he asked. I didn't want to lie to him.

'Well, we don't have any rods.'

'OK, then. That'll be eight dollars for the boat, please.'

Our vessel, a tatty-looking but robust rowing boat, had no engine and only two oars were provided. It was hard work in the heat to move the boat, but we both agreed we were certainly moving faster than we ever did when we were powered by the 13-horse-power engine across the Jordanelle Reservoir in Utah.

In what seemed no time at all we had travelled about three hundred yards and manoeuvred our craft into a small inlet on the other side of the lake. Here we could fish away from the prying eyes of the boat hire man who obviously had nothing better to do with his time and wouldn't look too kindly on our fishing without a permit, no matter how quirky the attempt. The extended recess of water was no longer than a hundred yards by thirty yards wide and the shade made the water look even darker. Dropping my line into the water, we began to paddle to wherever we saw bubbles emerge on the surface, which we considered a sure sign of aquatic life. Either that or the scorching temperature which was almost getting the better of us had begun to boil the water.

We decided to paddle towards the shade, on the assumption that this would also be the place the fish preferred to spend a warm summer's day. Unfortunately, as we manoeuvred the boat towards the end of the lake and the trees which would block the sun's rays, my line snagged on a branch which lay just under the surface and I lost my bait for the second time that afternoon. I reapplied a fresh piece, releasing the putrid smell once more, and

Bateman and I removed our T-shirts in an effort to combat the heat. All we could now do was wait.

'I spy with my little eye, something beginning with T,' Bateman said.

'Tree?'

'Yep.'

'Right, my turn. I spy with my little eye, something beginning with . . .' I had to make this one tricky to pass the time, '. . . M.'

'Mud,' Bateman answered instantly.

'Yeah. That was quick.'

I looked around. The problem with this game was that all we could see around us was water, trees, mud, insects and the boat. Unfortunately for a successful game of I Spy, everything began with different letters and we were hardly spoiled for choice. But at least the game had passed a minute or so – enough time for a fish to become attached to my line. I pulled my lasso out of the water. There was no fish on the end of the line but, surprisingly, the bait remained on the hook. As I dropped my line into the water in hope once more, the sound of a woodpecker came from the trees behind us and with it an idea for a different game.

'I hear with my little ear something beginning with W,' I said with a smile on my face, trying to look as if I was enjoying the entire experience. Bateman simply glared back at me with a kind of you-brought-me-here-in-a-thousand-degrees-and-now-you're-trying-to-make-me-play-this-stupid-game kind of way.

'Never mind. Shall we change location?'

'What's the point? We're not going to catch any-thing.'

Bateman's temper was somewhat frayed – probably because he had set up his own line and was losing bait as regularly as I was. The temperature, sweat, lack of success and the fact that we were five thousand miles from home floating in a lake in Tennessee for no other reason than to catch a fish with a lasso must have been getting to him.

'Just use a net,' he said.

'What?'

'Just use a net to catch the fish and I'll take a picture of you. No one will know the lasso wasn't used.'

'Bateman. Bateman, Bateman, Bateman,' I said, lift-ing my fingers to the bridge of my nose and shaking my head in an obvious attempt to stall for time to think of a great line. 'I can't cheat. If I do, our whole trip would be wasted. There would be no rules any more and if the world had no rules it would descend into chaos.'

'I've heard that line somewhere before.'

'Have you? I thought I just made it up.'

By now more than an hour had passed. I hadn't cheated and our little world remained on its fragile precipice, not yet fallen into bedlam through the wrongful use of a net. And then, out of nowhere, the most unexpected event occurred. I felt a gentle tug at the end of my line. I quickly wiped the sweat off my forehead, lifting my flip-flop off the excess rope and gripping the line with my hand. This was it. I pulled and tugged, and after a titanic struggle managed to take my first look at the branch my lasso had snared.

It was definitely time to go. The sun was at its peak and Bateman and I knew in our hearts that this law was doomed.

As we made our way back to the small wooden harbour where the rest of the six or seven rowing boats lay, I happened to catch a quick glimpse of the departure of the only other person fishing. I could clearly see her leaving her position by the lake completely empty-handed apart from her rod and flask. If she couldn't catch anything with a rod, what chance would I have had with a lasso?

We drove back through Memphis and continued into Mississippi, whose border lay less than ten miles south of the city. My new coupon book advised us that there was 'comfortable and affordable' accommodation in the little frontier town of Horn Lake. With a name like that, there was only one place Bateman wanted to eat.

'Let's go to Hooters!' It was becoming his catchphrase.

'Bateman, just because the name of the town is Horn Lake that doesn't mean it'll have a Hooters. It's only a small town.'

It must have been early evening when we arrived at Hooters in Horn Lake and found ourselves propping up the bar, being served by a waitress dressed in the quintessential Hooters uniform. Samantha was also at college but could easily have been a model and her scanty Hooters attire, I'm pleased to say, left little to the imagination. Our newest friend must have been about twenty-one years of age, had long blond hair, and struck a blow for the popular correlation of blond hair and intellect when she took a sudden liking to our driving licences which we had produced to prove our ages.

'Wow, they're pink. And what's this mean? Ours are nothing like these.'

Whether it was due to our undeniable charm, ravishing good looks or Bateman's promise to talk her through the history of the ancient symbolism of the DVLA, over the course of our two-hour drinking session we managed to secure a night on the town with Samantha and her friend after she had finished work.

'I'll pick you up around eleven at your motel, OK?'

'OK,' we replied excitedly in unison.

As our motel television, tuned to CNN, informed us that Hurricane Irene was on its way to North Carolina and would arrive in a matter of days (just about when we were due to arrive there, in fact), we were busy deciding what to wear and wondering if Samantha was even going to call. Maybe she had just invited us out so we would stop talking to her and leave the restaurant. Perhaps it was just a plan to get rid of us and we had taken the bait, unlike the numerous fish that allegedly lived in Poplar Tree. As Bateman spruced himself up, I kept reminding him that it was probably all a big waste of time and Samantha was never going to turn up. Just then the phone rang.

'She's outside!'

I can't say I remember much about the club. It was definitely in Memphis and I recall it took us about fifteen minutes to get there from the lobby of our motel. It was not the biggest club I've ever been to and it had a live band playing instead of the usual head-thumping repetitive beat I associate with dance clubs. Samantha's friend was called Kristin and had medium-length black hair and I would guess was somewhere in her early twenties. Both girls were excellent company and I was glad that now, away from Hooters where Samantha's job was to be pleasant to us, the girls were themselves and great people to be around. Every round Bateman bought came to over thirty dollars and I remember that when I purchased the same it came to under twenty. Goodness knows what Bateman was buying extra.

After more rounds than I would care to remember even if I could, the house lights of the club rose and we left the premises, walking back across the road to the car. Although we'd all had a bit to drink, Samantha was adamant that she'd been closely monitoring her alcohol consumption, and said she was perfectly capable of driving us back to the Mississippi border and Horn Lake. And we were too drunk to think about it too much. I must have fallen asleep, because before I knew it we had stopped in a shop's parking space just yards from our motel. Bateman was buying cigarettes, and as he left the shop I saw him do a double take at the car.

'Come look at this, Rich.'

Thinking Samantha might have some interesting roadkill jammed in the grille of her car, I leaped out and joined Bateman at the front. There was no cat spread across the tyre, no deer leg hanging out of the grille; not even a fly had smeared the windscreen.

'Look,' Bateman demanded.

Then it hit me, and no amount of alcohol could have alleviated the shock I felt as I surveyed the car's body, feeling instantly sober again. All holiday I'd been careful; the entire trip I'd been cautious and constantly aware. Yet when my defence was down, when drink had lowered my guard, I had allowed stupidity to breach my resistance: I had accepted a lift back to my motel with two girls I barely knew who were probably in no fit state to drive a car which was a positively unmistakable shade of red.

'It's red, Rich. The car's red.'

'Yes, I can see that, Bateman. I think I'll walk the last few yards.'

By the time I got back to our room, Bateman was impressing the girls by leaping off his bed and crashing down onto mine and then laughing at the ridiculous position he had landed in. Samantha greeted my entrance with a frown.

'What's so weird about my car being red?' she asked. Bateman explained and soon Samantha was wide-eyed with horror.

'Wow, that's weird. My God, that's spooky. I could have been killed or something.'

'No, I'm the one who was to be killed,' I pointed out helpfully.

'But I could have killed you. My car is red.' Samantha was quite obviously one of those girls who read horoscopes and believe every word.

'It doesn't matter. Look, nothing happened to me. I'm fine. That woman was just talking rubbish.' Samantha shook her head and stared at the ground. 'Bateman, just show her your driving licence. That'll cheer her up.'

I'm not sure if he did produce his licence to raise her morale, but whether he did or not the two disappeared beneath the covers of his bed leaving Kristin and me to do the same in mine. I couldn't help thinking what a pity it was that I hadn't met Kristin in San Francisco.

Checkout times are always cruel in motels, especially when you didn't get to sleep until well after the sun had risen. To me, the disappointment of the Tennessee fishing expedition was easily outweighed by the pleasure of the evening and the satisfaction of discovering that the charlatan in Long Beach was indeed just that. Her premonition that someone was going to offer me a lift in a red car might have come true, but her foreboding was thankfully misplaced. As Kristin and her friend left in Samantha's car, which in the clear visibility of the morning light gleamed a fantastic shade of pillar-box red, Bateman and I returned to our own car to test another of the psychic's forewarnings. Her premonition of a court case might not be too far from the truth as today we were going to drive to Oxford, Mississippi, where I hoped to see the front and back of a courthouse more than a hundred times. As we made our way back towards the interstate I looked at Bateman with a big smirk on my face.

'See, you were wrong. You thought I was going to die if I got into a red car. That woman said danger lurked and really the result was the exact opposite. I'm absolutely fine,' I boasted proudly.

Bateman turned in his seat and stared into my eyes.

'You don't know that. You could have caught something.'

14

It's Left, Left and Left Again

Ever since the game at Christmas and the extensive research that followed, I hadn't been able to wait to reach Oxford, Mississippi. The town was home to my favourite of all the laws I was in America to break – in Oxford, Mississippi it is illegal to drive round the town square more than a hundred times in a single session. Brilliance, sheer brilliance. It's a law which practically defines stupidity and pointlessness.

As we made our way into the centre of the town, the leafy neighbourhoods gave way to a sudden avenue of shops which culminated at a T-junction where I could only turn right. I'd seen the place before during my Internet research of the town and recognized it instantly.

'This is it, Bateman.'

There, standing in front of me, was the Lafayette

County courthouse, which was the centrepiece of the town square. The rectangular white building with its mighty Doric pillars and pristine European-style clock tower stood behind a confederate statue which I decided would make a superb starting and finishing line for the Oxford Grand Prix. Although I hadn't planned on breaking the law until later on in the evening, I got a good idea of what to expect as Bateman and I made four laps to find a vacant parking space.

Oxford was named after the English city as part of an ultimately successful campaign to persuade the University of Mississippi to locate its main campus here. Ole Miss, as the university is more commonly known, now enrols more than 16,500 students, and during term time the population of this affluent town in a poor area more than doubles. In mid-August, the 12,000 permanent residents, plus Bateman and me, were free to explore the town in almost perfect peace. I was also excited to learn that William Faulkner grew up in the town after moving from nearby New Albany when he was five. Sadly, my excitement was short-lived when I realized I was confusing the author of classics such as *The Sound and the Fury* and *As I Lay Dying* with the actor who played Columbo, named Peter Falk, and that the statue of the man, which sits on a bench outside City Hall, was not of a cigar-wielding detective in a trench coat asking for 'just one more thing'.

The shops surrounding the square are archetypal of

small-town America and the topiary gardens which straddle the sidewalks and encircle lampposts make the exploration of the town a thoroughly enjoyable activity. Antique shops, bookstores with cafés upstairs and Neilson's, a department store almost unchanged since 1897, are delightful assets to a town where quaintness seems if anything overemphasized. The pleasing if incongruous winding streets and the bizarre features such as the old-fashioned English telephone box in the north-east corner of the square (dedicated, the plaque informed us, by John and Laura Valentine from Oxfordshire) are not enough to disguise the town's shameful past.

In 1962, Oxford was the scene of one of the most brutal displays of racial hatred ever witnessed in the state. When James Meredith was allowed to enrol as the first black student at Ole Miss after eighteen months of legal and political wrangling, local fury erupted when Meredith was smuggled in by federal troops for his first day. The town square riot, in which bottles and rocks were thrown at the military personnel, left three people dead and 160 injured. Despite constant threats, Meredith graduated a year later and as a defiant gesture wore a 'NEVER' badge (the segregationist slogan of Governor Ross Barnett) upside down. Was it because of the riots that the law about driving in the town square existed, or was it brought in earlier? This was one statute I definitely wanted to know more about. It just seemed too strange that such a thing would be passed. Surely anyone could drive round the square as many times as they wished? Or were they under constant scrutiny by the police, who were just waiting for the conclusion of the 101st lap? With no obvious library on the town square in which to conduct my research, I visited a resplendent bookshop by the name of Square Books, just opposite the start-finish line, whose upstairs café would act as a perfect grandstand for the proceedings later on that day. I was informed that the town was home to two libraries, the superior facility being located on the Oxford University campus less than a mile from the square.

With the academic year not restarting for another eight weeks, the campus felt like a ghost town. Normally the quiet roads and empty Greek revival-style buildings which surrounded me would be bustling with thousands of students clutching folders and textbooks in a mad dash to arrive for lectures in time.

The woman on the front desk in Ole Miss's library directed me downstairs to where someone would be able to help. From there I was sent to the upper floor of the building, back down to ground level and then to the other side of the room where, after my fifth embarrassing explanation, I was directed to the law library on the other side of the campus.

'Stuff this; I'm going to wait in the car.' I think Bateman had the right idea.

Behind the front desk of the law library sat the only person, other than me, in the entire building. Waking him up, I asked if he knew anything about the origin of the law or whether it was still in use today. He shrugged his shoulders, laughed and presented me with the Oxford, Mississippi city ordinance book.

'If it is it'll be in here.'

Thirty minutes after sitting down and opening the thousand-page file and reading the sections on traffic, peaceful protest, automobiles and miscellaneous, I was out of ideas. If the law did feature, it was well hidden somewhere in the other 900-odd pages. Besides, I already knew exactly what it was going to say, and the file would have given me no clue as to its origin or background.

When I joined Bateman back at the car, it was agreed that we would begin the laps at seven that evening, after we had returned to our motel and slept off our hangovers.

I never did get any sleep that afternoon and instead created a tally chart and checklist on which Bateman could record the laps and any events of interest which occurred. By six o'clock we had made our way to the town square with a full tank of gas.

The 206-metre course was a simple one and was hardly in the same league as Brands Hatch or Le Mans. It did, however, have pedestrians to be wary of and wasn't as square as the name suggested. The Oxford Grand Prix track wasn't even rectangular in shape and actually consisted of six mini-straights in an obscure hexagonal design – unfortunately disqualifying it from featuring in *America's Greatest Roundabouts*. Luckily, the 'square' was devoid of any sort of traffic lights or traffic-calming systems, so laps could be completed with relative ease. The confederate statue was selected as my start line due to the fact that a pedestrian crossing marked the road between it and the bookshop I had visited earlier. Three other similar crossings were frequently used by the residents to traverse the 'track' to the east, north and west of the square. After the first corner, an easy left took us to the rear of the courthouse and the junction of Lamar Boulevard, where the road widened to allow for the flow of added traffic and the longest of the pedestrian crossings was to be found. So that was the course. Hardly one which would inspire the NASCAR organizers to relocate the Indy 500 or one that Bernie Ecclestone is likely to wish to use for Formula One training, but it was a track where I had reserved pole position and on which I would definitely not be lapped.

Traffic lights would have been nice for the start of the event, but in their absence we made do with a woman who had positioned herself with an easel by her side and was painting a picture of the scene south of the courthouse where the road leading to the square is met by both Square Books and the row of trees which leads to the university campus. I was hoping she was drawing a chequered flag to present to us when we crossed the line after completing lap 101 but I didn't have time to tell her about my attempt before

Bateman began the stopwatch on his mobile phone and we were off.

From a standing start, I didn't expect a great deal from lap 1, but it would be a good benchmark from which to assess the times of following circuits. With a couple of cars joining me on 'telephone turn' which stood at the rear of the courthouse where Jackson Avenue widened the track, I completed my virgin lap with a respectable time of 32 seconds. Lap 2, without the hindrance of a standing start, was obviously going to be quicker and even with the interference of a pedestrian crossing usage I recorded a time of under half a minute. It wasn't until lap 12, the fastest lap so far, that I felt as if the law wouldn't take as long as I had once thought to break: it was the first lap without interruptions of any nature, and it set a course record of 25 seconds. Only eight laps later disaster struck: two cars joining the square had held me up before an entire family used the third of the pedestrian crossings to further delay my progress to the line on a lap which took 40 seconds to complete.

Lap 30 brought about a new fastest lap (24 seconds) and the departure of the woman and her easel from the statue. Several circuits beforehand, a man had joined her, and as they left, hand in hand, the woman took one final look at our car. Even concentrating on her work, she must have seen it over twenty times and surely must have included it in her painting as a permanent feature of Oxford town centre's scenic landscape.

By lap 34, the scenery was beginning to become a tad repetitive. 'Telephone turn' was home to the First Bank and the City Hall, and after crossing the line I passed such noticeable landmarks as a pub with upper decking for a perfect view of my progress, and Duvall's, the original home of the First National Bank of Oxford founded by Faulkner's grandfather. It was probably because of my interest in my surroundings and my lack of attention to pedestrians and other hazards that the lap ended with a new fastest time of 23 seconds – a record which would stand for the remainder of the day. Back in the mood for speed and with a record to break, I was disappointed when the following valiant lap was ruined by the presence of a barrage of pedestrians and the police. I wasn't too shocked at their presence and my slight anxiety was quickly laid to rest when I realized that neither of the law enforcers was dressed in a bullet-proof vest or took obvious exception to our flag.

It wasn't until lap 52 that the police made their presence felt again, but with the cops only completing half a lap and continuing down Van Buren Avenue, I was free to complete the remaining 49 laps without the need for a pit-stop.

This was the only time when the law-breaking was somewhat dull. The halfway point brought a minor celebration but it simply meant we still had fifty revolutions to go. Fast laps were now few and far between and after clocking times of 28, 29 and even 32 seconds, I was beginning to wonder just how many lives I had endangered to produce the record. Bateman, who by now had resigned himself to the all-important job of tallying up the laps, sat quietly in the passenger seat hoping something diversionary would happen. I was happy for lap records and early into the course was thrilled with claiming them or narrowly missing out on the honour by a second or two, but I could tell Bateman was bored. To him, the prospect of circling the courthouse in a quicker time than before by a second or two was getting duller by the circuit. He was probably paying close attention to the passing businesses, hoping to catch a glimpse of a Hooters he hadn't spotted on the previous fifty laps, the only thing keeping him awake.

After sixty laps, I half expected to have some sort of fan base who knew what we were doing or had at least noticed that we had passed them dozens of times and would maybe wave to us on each lap from now on. But ever since the lady with the easel had left the square, not a single person had shown that they had noticed us passing them several times or raised an eyebrow at our ubiquitous presence. It wasn't until lap 82 that a couple seated on a bench to the east of the courthouse opposite the pedestrian crossing indicated that they had definitely noticed our frequent appearances. After passing them two or three times as we approached the final fifteen laps, I felt as if we now dominated their conversation. Before, it had looked as if the two were in a very deep and meaningful conversation, maintaining eye contact at all times; now they had changed position completely and were directing baffled looks at the middle of the road and pointing at our car as we raced by. Whatever they had been talking about before, it was definitely not what they were discussing now.

'Louise, I love you and I've never felt this way about anyone in my life. We've been together now for over six years and I've finally plucked up the courage to do this. I'm going to ask you one very important question. Louise . . . is it me or has that car passed us more than ten times already?' OK. Maybe it wasn't as important as that but you never know.

As far as they were aware, the two madmen in the blue car had driven past them more than a dozen times. Little did they know that these 'madmen' were well on their way to their ninetieth revolution. Yet we were hardly discreet or inconspicuous. I'm willing to bet that not only in Oxford or Mississippi that day, but in the entire continent of North America – or maybe even the world – we were the only drivers of a Dodge Neon with a Union Jack on the antenna and a flag of St Piran spread out on the parcel shelf.

The last five laps were riddled with the threat of pedestrians and cars forcing their way onto the course, doing nothing for my thirst for lap records. With a final lap time of 32 seconds we crossed the line of lap 101 without the waving of a chequered flag or any presentation of champagne. Even the perplexed couple, possibly reluctant to come into closer contact with a pair of certifiable lunatics, quickly left the town square walking in the opposite direction to our parked car.

The total time for all 101 laps and therefore the completion of the entire law-break was 52 minutes and 19 seconds. That, for the statisticians amongst us, resulted in an average lap time of 31.08 seconds, which, as I'm sure you've already worked out, is an average speed of 14.8 miles per over the laps, which totalled 13 miles in all. The most important datum to me was the fact that after failure in Tennessee, the drive that had taken almost an hour to complete represented the fifteenth law I had attempted to break and the ninth in which I was victorious. That in itself was a reason to celebrate, and although I wasn't planning on shaking up the entire contents of a Formula One podium-sized bottle of bubbly, at least there was a bar we could enjoy a small tipple in.

15

Watery Graves

For only the third time in the holiday I was awake early enough the morning after the epic Grand Prix to experience the culinary delights of the motel's 'continental breakfast'. As always, the choice of what to eat was limited to bagels, apples and a fine array of breakfast cereals, and I entered alone as Bateman had long ago dubbed the meal 'continental shit' – see what he did there?

It was, however, the first time that I had eaten with no other guests around, leaving me on my own to wait for the bagel to pop out of the toaster. I had enjoyed meeting and conversing with Joye's Honduran mother in Phoenix and had had a delightfully peculiar encounter after my appearance on the Wank and O'Brien Show with a family from Surrey who had travelled down from Canada and stayed overnight in Indianapolis in order to attend a folk music festival in Ohio. But in Oxford there was no one to chat to, and not a soul wanted to hear my lap-by-lap commentary of the previous evening's crime. Unbelievable.

Finishing my bagel and toast, I was then left with the tricky decision of which beverage to wash it down with. I opted for the milk, stored in an industrial-sized container. Lowering my cup and holding it in place beneath the tap, I pulled lightly on the handle until a sufficient amount had been dispensed. I noticed that the flow of milk continued for several seconds after I had returned the handle to its original position. As I stepped away from the machine, still watching the dribble from the tap, the handle which had just left my hand fell to the floor. Shit.

Milk began to gush out of the small plastic tube to which the handle had been connected, soaking my shorts and T-shirt and pouring on to the floor. Not wanting to act like a coward (or get caught for it, as I was the only person in the dining room and would definitely cop the blame), I couldn't simply run away from the danger zone, leaving whoever entered the breakfast room after my departure to face a titanic struggle against a strong current of pasteurized milk in order to get to their morning bagel. I quickly grabbed the fallen handle and did what any decent citizen, or indeed tourist, would do – I placed it back over the tubing so delicately that whoever used it next was guaranteed to restart the torrential flow of white liquid and consider themselves the guilty party. Well, it worked when I was younger. Unfortunately, no sooner had the handle been precisely manoeuvred into place, with only the smallest of drops emerging from the tap, than it dramatically sprang back to life. I managed to grip the tubing with my fingers until the flow had ceased, but not before further gallons of milk had saturated the carpet. Now I was faced with a dilemma. Should I keep hold of the tubing until someone appeared (bearing in mind that I hadn't seen anyone since I woke up that morning) or run out of the room like a bat out of hell, leaving the container to empty its load and turn the breakfast room into a reservoir of milk? Luckily the decision was made for me by the appearance of one of the cleaners.

'Excuse me. I could do with a bit of a hand here. I've kind of broken the handle of the milk container. I tried to fix it.' The cleaner looked at the floor, the handle and the four bowls of milk on the drenched work surface, which were surrounded by the sodden corn flakes I had used in an earlier attempt to dam the semi-skimmed waterfall. 'Um ... but I couldn't,' I added, as if the state of the room wasn't sufficient evidence.

'Just go and contact the manager for me, will you?'

I eventually tracked the manager down to the front desk, but had to wait until he had finished an important phone call before I could break the rather disturbing milk-related news to him. By the time he finally ran to the rescue, the hapless cleaner had been holding the plastic tubing for well over ten minutes.

Back on the road, and with a new pair of shorts, it was time to concentrate on our next destination. Because the interstate which would have taken us to Birmingham, Alabama was still under construction, constant detours took Bateman and me through small-town Alabama, including such wonderfully named places as Natural Bridge and Brilliant. Thinking a detour might improve my chances of breaking another law, I referred to my book of laws and flicked straight to Alabama, where I made quite an interesting discovery.

'Hey, Bateman. Did you know that in an attempt to cut down on the number of laws that governed them, the residents of Brooksville, Alabama applied to be governed by no other laws than the Ten Commandments?'

'Really? What *are* the Ten Commandments, anyway?'

'Um, thou shall not steal . . .'

'Murder?'

'Yeah, thou shall not kill. Thou shall not have any other God but me or something like that, adultery, keep the Sabbath day holy and five others.'

'They're in the Bible, aren't they?' asked Bateman.

'Yeah. Old Testament, I think.'

'We'll look them up in one of those Gideon Bibles we always find in our motel when we get one.'

'Yeah, sure. At least it can't spray me with milk.'

For a second, I thought that the five remaining commandments would supply enough incentive for the start of another of our own specially devised travel games. That was until Bateman spotted the remains of a racoon which had somehow managed to impale itself on the raised cornerstone of the sidewalk.

As the sun began to fall in the sky, it was obvious we were going to have to spend the night in the state of Georgia, a few hundred miles short of our next destination of Spartanburg in South Carolina. The decision to stay overnight in Atlanta was precipitated by the weather, which was rapidly deteriorating: suddenly the heavy rain striking the windscreen was more than the wipers could deal with. Following articulated lorries was a death trap, but passing them became impossible owing to the abundance of water which collected on the outside of the glass. The horrific driving conditions continued for well over an hour. By then the road was submerged under several inches of water in places, and reminded me of both the severe storms we had fallen victim to in Globe and my dreaded milk incident earlier in the day. I began to wonder whether this was divine revenge for our blasphemy and/or lack of knowledge of the Ten Commandments. Thankfully, we managed to make it to a motel at the top of a hill (just in case), and the second Bateman had left to find somewhere to drink and I had turned on the television the lightning which had joined the rain totally knocked out the TV signal, leaving me with a screen which resembled our windscreen during the severest part of the storm. As I lay on my bed with curtains ajar I could see that the lightning was becoming very frequent and almost as regular as clockwork. Nearly every three or four seconds, out the corner of my eye and through the slight gap in the curtains, the flashes were sharp and luminous against the night sky, and I couldn't help but open the door of the room to properly witness such a sight. I stood at the top of the outdoor stairs and waited for the next crack of atmospheric electricity. Surprisingly it never arrived, and as I turned back towards the door, wondering how lightning which was so frequent could simply stop, I noticed that above the window of our room was a faulty light which flicked on and off incessantly. Not lightning.

Thinking my chance of entertainment that evening had vanished, I decided to use the laptop Bateman had bought in Salt Lake City to check and send some emails. Sitting in my inbox was an email from Dave O'Brien, who had replied to the message I had sent him thanking him for inviting us onto his show. His reply, however, was of particular interest, since it turned out that Bateman had sent Dave his own message, leaving his email address, to which he hoped the intern who had first greeted us (whose name both he and I had forgotten) would reply. Bateman planned to spend an additional two weeks in America after I had flown home, and therefore I felt it was now up to me, being the kind-hearted friend that I am, to create a fake email address and attempt to make him fly back to Indianapolis to a girl who didn't exist. Indianaradiogirl@hotmail.com was plucked from thin air and the intern – whose real name was Angela – was now known as 'Lisa Jennings'. Any doubts in my mind that this was a cruel trick to play on my friend were quickly banished when I emailed Dave about what I was doing and he replied that it was the 'funniest thing he'd heard all day'. After sending an email to Bateman asking why he wanted 'me' to get in touch I left the room and went in search of my friend. It didn't take long. By this stage of the holiday Bateman appeared to have developed a sixth sense, or acquired an acute sense of smell, which could lead him quite effortlessly to the nearest Hooters from anywhere within a four-mile radius.

I hadn't shaved for over a week, and next morning I began to shave only the stubble which had grown on my cheeks and the top of my neck, leaving the facial hair on my chin and upper lip well alone. In just under two weeks, Bateman and I intended to be arriving in Boston, Massachusetts – a state where goatees were strictly forbidden. From this point onward, the beard would be carefully cultivated in preparation for our arrival.

That day, for the first and last time on the holiday, we entered the fast-food restaurant known as McDonald's. Skyy, the cashier, found Bateman's accent hilarious.

'I love your accent. What's your name?' she asked in a deep southern drawl.

'Luke.'

'Say it again.'

'Luke.'

'Hang on one second.' Skyy left her position behind the till and returned seconds later, dragging a male colleague by the collar. 'Listen to this man say his name. Say it again.'

'Luke.'

'Isn't that so funny?' asked Skyy, holding her sides and leaning towards her colleague in expectation of agreement.

'Don't worry, she's on drugs,' he remarked and with a straight face took Bateman's order. I was given no reason not to believe him.

If any organization were to sponsor this crime spree I imagine it would have to be Wal-Mart. Whenever I needed any sort of apparatus to aid me in my illicit adventures, they had always come up trumps. Wal-Mart, Spartanburg was certainly no exception, and Bateman and I left the store in search of Magnolia Cemetery armed with a slice of watermelon. You guessed it: in Spartanburg, South Carolina it is illegal to eat a watermelon in the cemetery. And not only in Spartanburg. With the exception of laws which outlaw spitting on sidewalks and the carrying of ice creams in your back pocket, laws pertaining to the eating of watermelon in specific areas were by far the most common across states all over America. Beech Grove, Indiana has a similar decree. The only problem was that it was Sunday and there were no Chambers of Commerce open to help us find our way to the cemetery. I took a nervous bite out of the melon.

With no other course of action available to us, we simply drove around Spartanburg in the hope that sooner or later we would come across the cemetery. A series of lucky guesses landed us on Magnolia Street and we cut our speed down, keeping our eyes peeled for any sort of grassland or area which resembled a graveyard. A railroad and three crossroads later, Magnolia Street finally ended at the junction of Church and Dewey.

'How could we have missed it? The road's only about half a mile long,' I cried.

'Perhaps it's further down that way.' Bateman pointed back down the road. 'We might not have joined the road at the beginning.'

We turned the car round and drove back the way we had come. We had almost reached the point at which we had originally joined the road when I spotted something.

'How the hell did we miss that?' I shouted.

Between two eight-foot brick towers was a metal archway more than twenty feet high, which, the framework stated, was the entrance to Magnolia Cemetery. Ironically, the cemetery was positioned a block away from the Spartanburg County Judicial Center and opposite the sheriff's office in whose parking lot were more than forty stationary squad cars. None of my previous law-breakings had been so open to police scrutiny as in Spartanburg.

The cemetery itself was set in open woodland with a single railway track running alongside, and the state of the graves was abysmal. Never in my life had I seen vandalism on quite the same scale as in Magnolia Cemetery and, as always, I began to speculate on the history of this bizarre law. Maybe it was simply designed to discourage pip-spitting, but since the cemetery had clearly been neglected for decades that didn't seem to make much sense. The few headstones which remained in the ground and did not litter the pathways like parts of a jigsaw puzzle were still in a terrible condition and had been either poorly pieced back together or bore giant cracks where chunks of granite were missing. Where walls once existed, crumbling segments of piled stone now stood, and memorial statues lay on their sides until it appeared that no grave had been spared indignity. In the centre of the cemetery, the list of the deceased remained perfectly intact. If the condition of my surroundings wasn't enough to make me hurry up and eat the fruit, there was the chilling fact that with thirteen graves bearing my family moniker, Smith was by far the most frequently represented name in the graveyard.

I must admit, this was the one law I did not enjoy breaking. Originally, I had envisaged a picnic in the centre of the cemetery involving watermelon sandwiches, watermelon pie, and watermelon vodka with which to wash it all down. This was the first time that the comic appeal of the whole adventure had been lost – like the memories of the people who were buried around me. I devoured the slice of watermelon quickly, and we returned to the car. En route we passed a crypt whose door was dented and hanging off its hinges, most evidently ajar. Not a word was spoken between Bateman and me until we were on the road again, when Bateman pointed out what was on both our minds.

'How can a cemetery so close to a police station be so bad?'

Attempting to rub the remaining watermelon juice into my T-shirt as I drove, I totted up our scores so far. Although the law was the sixteenth I had attempted to break, it was the tenth success. The crime spree had finally reached double figures, and when I used the laptop later on, after Bateman had checked his emails, a further cause for celebration appeared in the form of his reply to 'Lisa'. Apparently I was the best-looking girl he had ever seen in his life. Lucky me.

16

Doggy Paddle

On a historic day when Israeli troops made their final withdrawal from the Gaza Strip thirty-eight years after capturing the narrow coastal area, and a day after the Iraqi constitution deadline was extended, the front pages of the morning's national newspapers were dominated by the rather disturbing news that petrol prices in America had reached their highest ever level at three dollars a gallon! Three dollars? Nearly half what we paid in England? How outrageous! How can the American government live with themselves after raising taxes on oil prices to such a level? How could they sleep at night? Unlike the American public, Bateman and I felt a deep sense of jealousy and amazement at what the Americans saw as daylight robbery and what we could only dream about happening at home.

It had been two days since the watermelon eating in Spartanburg and now we were as far north as Virginia where speed radars were outlawed and, the signs warned, speed violations were detected by aircraft. How exciting. The next law-break was to be either in Washington, D.C. or in Ocean City in Maryland. In order not to double back on ourselves we decided to go to Ocean City first, driving to the east of Virginia and taking the bridge across Chesapeake Bay. Fortunately, this also meant we wouldn't have to travel through West Virginia where it was perfectly legal to scrape roadkill off the road and take it home for supper. With Bateman's eagle eye for the tarmac-assisted delicacy, I wasn't too keen on what might be rustled up for our evening meal.

At the south-east corner of mainland Virginia, facing the southernmost tip of a peninsula made up of parts of Delaware, Maryland and Virginia itself, is the delightfully English-sounding town of Norfolk. We had already driven through Suffolk, Portsmouth and the counties of Isle of Wight, Southampton and Sussex. Everything in Virginia seemed to sound English, and the areas of Norfolk we passed through during the drive to the downtown area, where high-rise buildings stared down at the yachts and boats drifting alongside each other close to our motel, all exuded prosperity. It felt as if we were back in rich and powerful America once again, and the awe-inspiring bridge we would cross to reach the peninsula, on our way to Ocean City, was proof of the city's affluence and America's engineering ingenuity.

It may not be the most well known of America's landmarks, and in fact I hadn't heard of it until the name appeared on the map, but the Chesapeake Bay Bridge is a modern feat of engineering prowess. So it might not be as well known as the Seven Mile Bridge which winds its way down the chain of the Florida Keys on its way to Key West, or as famous as the Brooklyn Bridge which links Manhattan Island to its suburban neighbour, but what distinguishes Chesapeake – other than the confusion it generates by looking a lot like 'cheapskate' – is its dramatic appearance. It is a work of distinctive and stylish elegance which would make Isambard Kingdom Brunel and other great visionaries sit up in their graves and take note.

When it was first constructed in 1964, the bridge spanning the twenty-three miles between south-eastern Virginia and the Delmarva Peninsula was officially named after civic leader Lucias J. Kellam Jr. Its ingenuity lies in the fact that although the bridge stands less than thirty feet above the ocean strait, ships and boats which require a greater elevation in order to pass underneath needn't worry. After the first several miles, the bridge comes to an end on a man-made island where a tunnel, plummeting deep under the water, allows the road to continue beneath the sea for over a mile, permitting the unhampered crossing of nautical traffic far above. The concrete, man-made islands, of which there are four in all, are each slightly larger than five acres, and one has a gift shop and restaurant to encourage tourists to stand and stare at the engineering marvel around them.

Back on terra firma, the peninsula was a huge contrast to the shore we had just left and looked more like the ends of the earth. The skyscrapers which lined Norfolk and Virginia Beach's coast did not extend to this side of the water and the multitude of cars alongside which we had been squeezed on the bridge had suddenly eerily disappeared, leaving us more or less alone on a quiet stretch of road where trees and the occasional house predominated, though we noticed a couple of shops which seemed to specialize in fireworks or peanuts and a couple more which combined the two.

Sixty miles north, just as the narrow stretch of land widened, we entered Maryland – the nineteenth state we had visited thus far. I wasn't sure what to expect from Ocean City – according to the map it was just a simple dot, and without the colouring which is used to indicate a great deal of urbanization, or any nearby interstates, I imagined the town would be a quiet, peaceful haven. I couldn't have been more wrong.

The sparse housing and dilapidated appearance of the businesses we passed as we headed towards the coast are deceptive. Ocean City is situated at the southern tip of a narrow strip of land only four blocks wide; 146th Street, over seven miles north, rests exactly on the Maryland–Delaware border. Thanks to the city's post-war boom and the importing of tonnes of dune sand to form a picturesque beach, the strip is now home to bars, restaurants and numerous hotels, and all manner of activities from mini-golf and banana-boat rides to horse racing and the local Ripley's Believe It or Not Museum await your discovery. Far from being a tiny Maryland backwater, Ocean City is one of the most popular vacation spots in the east. Unfortunately, Bateman and I were not in the mood for jollity and excitement and had hit a very uncommunicative patch in our holiday – after thirty-three days of constant companionship, conversations tended to grind to a halt with short, one-word answers or grunts. I hadn't even dared mention the dead bird I saw lying on the side of the road earlier in the afternoon, squandering a point in the game for fear of his response.

Arriving in a tourist hub in mid-August meant that, despite my coupon book, no cheap motel deals were to be found in the town and Bateman's mood – which was a combined result of lack of sleep and drinking the previous evening – made him a less-than-patient travelling partner.

'A hundred and sixty-nine dollars a night they were asking for in there! I walked right out!' I said as I returned to the car yet again. 'Don't know why there aren't any coupons; there are loads of hotels.'

'Yeah, well not everyone's a gyppo like you!'

'Yes, Bateman. I'm a gypsy,' I remarked sarcastically.

'Things are more expensive on the coast, you know?'

'Are they?' I replied, upping the ante on the sarcasm.

'It is the summer.'

'Couldn't tell by the clouds though, could you?' I replied, trying to break the tension.

'It's still in the eighties!' Bateman snapped.

With the majority of hotels and motels asking for well over $150, we made our way back over the bridge onto the mainland and West Ocean City.

Leaving Bateman to sleep off his hangover in the hope that his mood would improve, I made my way across the road from our motel and into the Ocean City Tourist Office in which I checked my and 'Lisa's' emails. There being no reply awaiting me in 'Lisa's' inbox, and with little else to do to keep myself entertained, I returned to the motel, grabbed my towel and headed for the pool for a swim on my own.

After a dozen or so peaceful and calming lengths, the silence was suddenly broken by the arrival of two children who jumped in and started floating around on body boards. Like most Americans, these boys had been raised to be polite, and, in no way shy, they instantly introduced themselves. John and Joshua weren't identical twins but they looked the same, had similar haircuts and were equally overweight. In our brief conversation, I learned that they both wanted to grow up to become cops, and had 'never met a guy from where I was from' before. As I pushed myself off the wall of the pool to begin another length, John began to read the rules of the pool out loud.

'No running or diving; no eating or drinking around the pool; children under the age of fourteen must be . . .' The word was 'accompanied' and John looked over to see if his brother was looking. He wasn't. '. . . um, watched by an adult.'

'Accompanied,' said a bold voice from over the fence. 'The word is accompanied, son.'

The man with the teacher's instinct entered the pool area and turned out to be the children's granddad, who had come to join his grandchildren with his wife by his side. John and Joshua introduced me to him, and when he entered the pool we began chatting.

Dwight was an elderly gentleman who was holidaying with two generations of his family from West Virginia, and was very quick to dispel any opinion I might have formed about his relatives.

'Hey, Rich, I've got four grandchildren. My two little girls are straight-A students' – he pointed at the twins – 'and I've also got Dumb and Dumber over there.'

Talking to Dwight was interesting, to say the least. He was blithe and totally at ease – which you have to be when hobnobbing with a total stranger in a swimming pool wearing just a pair of shorts. Liz, his wife, who by now had managed to enter the pool, seemed to know her place and stood at a distance and simply agreed with every point her husband made whenever Dwight went into earnest mode.

'So, are you a religious man?' he asked.

'Um, no, not really. England tends to be more

populated by non-churchgoers nowadays,' I replied. Dwight shook his head disappointedly.

'Shame that. You've got God versus Darwin over there, haven't you?'

'Pardon?' I asked, thinking I was missing an epic, not-to-be-missed heavyweight title fight.

'People either praise God or Darwin.'

'Oh, Charles Darwin – *Origin of Species* man. Well, I wouldn't say that. People believe his work but he's not seen as a god.'

'All that talk of us evolving from apes. I never used to be no monkey.'

Dwight and his wife were creationists, and ever since I had learned of the theology, I had wanted to meet a believer. Basically, Creationism is the belief that the universe was created by a supernatural being or through a deity's supernatural intervention. The creed is almost always coupled with a strong religious conviction in the believer and Dwight certainly had that.

'But there's evidence to back Darwin up. What have you got – holy scriptures?' I asked.

Dwight and his wife scoffed at the suggestion of anything so preposterous. 'Recently they found a bit of Noah's Ark, so that proves the Bible is true, doesn't it?'

'Not really,' I replied. '*If* they found it and *if* it was part of Noah's Ark, then surely it means that that part of the Bible has some truth to it – not all of it.'

In Dwight's case, a belief in Creationism was sadly

accompanied by some more blatantly right-wing credos on everything from terrorism and politics to immigration, including the opinion that Cubans and Mexicans choose to come to America because it's the greatest nation on earth and not, as I pointed out, because it's the closest.

'Abraham Lincoln once said that this country will fall from within. That's exactly what it's doing. This country has too much anger – everyone hates each other. Even my son's in jail,' he remarked.

'Oh, yeah? Is he?' I replied tentatively.

'Yeah. He shot his wife . . .' he said quite breezily, and paused before adding, '. . . and her boyfriend.'

'Really?'

'Yeah, lucky he survived . . . she didn't.' Dwight slumped and stared into the pool water before releasing his anger. 'And they sued me!'

'Why?' By this point I was stepping carefully back away from him.

'He borrowed my rifle to shoot her with. I'm telling ya, Rich, anyone can be a cop over here. You don't have to be clever.'

'Is that right?' I replied, turning to John and Joshua who by now were trying to climb on the same body board. 'Tell me again what you two want to be when you grow up?'

'My name's John and he's Joshua,' John replied.

Dwight shook his head and extended his arm in their direction as if he were unveiling his future descendants. 'See what I mean?'

*

By the time Bateman had arisen from his comatose state, which seemed to have cured his mood, the sun had set and the law-breaking would have to wait until the following day. Tonight we were to experience the life and soul of Ocean City, but first we had to drive to the park-and-ride car park on our side of the bridge which seemed to be the only viable option for crossing in the evenings. The Ocean City bus station was situated near the end of the pier, where everything was reminiscent of the British seaside – minus litter, drunkards and donkey shit on the beach. A Ferris wheel stood forlornly abandoned, shut down for the night, just like the corkscrew roller coaster alongside. In full swing were the energetically lit amusement arcades, and food carts lined the boardwalk to the beach. To complete the all-British seaside experience, the heavens opened and we ran to the nearest bar for shelter.

'Two beers, please,' Bateman ordered, and we were asked for our picture ID as is the case in any bar, restaurant or venue which serves alcoholic beverages. We reached into our wallets and produced our UK driving licences.

'Sorry, boys, it has to be a US driver's licence.'

'Why?' we asked. Every other place in America had accepted our licences as proof of our age.

'Sorry, guys, it's bar policy.'

So we couldn't drink in that bar. Big deal. There were plenty of others on the same street and we only had to run out into the rain for less than a minute to find one. A doorman stopped us as we tried to enter.

'Can I see some ID, please, boys?' We proffered our licences once more and met with a similar response.

'You don't have US driver's licences, do you?'

'How the hell can we have US driving licences when we're English? Do you expect us to pass our US driving test before we come?' Bateman wasn't best pleased as we walked away.

'What's wrong with my driving licence? It's better than yours. Can you drive anywhere in the world with your driving licence? No. I bloody can!'

The bar where we made our third attempt at wetting our whistles had an Irishman on the door and surely that guaranteed victory.

'ID please,' he said.

'OK, but I warn you. They're UK driving licences,' I replied.

'Sorry, boys. The manager won't allow these. They have to be American.'

'But you're Irish, you know these are real. What's wrong with this city? You don't live here, do you?'

'God no,' he replied.

Before we decided to buy cans and return to the motel, we tried one final bar. Thankfully, the guy accepted our IDs and didn't care less what country they were from. As we discussed the difficulty we had endured in our quest for a drink, a Romanian waitress who stood by the door handing out menus and show-ing people to their tables leaned over to offer her expert opinion on why the Americans had not believed our ID was genuine. 'Because zey are stoopid.'

After a few drinks and an evening's free entertainment supplied by a magician, we returned to the motel, where Bateman requested I drop him back in town with his passport. 'Now we'll see who won't let me in, won't we? Bastards.'

In Ocean City it is illegal to eat whilst swimming and the following day the conditions were perfect for such an activity. The previous night's rain had subsided and been replaced by clear blue skies and temperatures in the upper thirties again. We had ground to make up today and this law was hopefully going to be the quickest one yet. At the food stand opposite Ripley's Believe It or Not Museum I purchased what can only be described as the smallest, and at four dollars the most expensive, hot dog in existence and made my way towards the beach. Although I wasn't impressed by the size of the hot dog, the seagull which followed me all the way across the pier and down onto the pristine white sands of the beach certainly was and kept ogling the food with criminal intent. Maybe he thought I was a city boy, or someone from inland who would be an easy target from whom to filch a free hot dog, but he knew nothing of my background.

'You think you're going to steal my hot dog, do ya? I know your tricks; I'm from Cornwall, you know. I've been to St Ives where hundreds of your friends live. Don't think I don't know what you're up to,' I warned him.

Undeterred, the bird remained on my tail until I chased him back up the beach in a desperate bid to show him who was boss. With the seagull out of the picture, Bateman and I were free to prepare for the law-breaking. After I had quickly placed a towel round my waist and changed into my swimming shorts, Bateman guarded our things while I made my way into the sea, hot dog in hand. The surf conditions weren't the greatest for swimming: choppy, three to four-foot waves broke haphazardly, and the lifeguards' whistles sounded every time a swimmer drifted perilously close to the pier's wooden structure. I strolled into the water, dropped my shoulders to meet the breaking waves, and decided it was time to place the hot dog in my mouth. I began with a touch of breaststroke, and received a strange look from the lady I greeted as I passed.

'Goob mormin,' I mumbled incomprehensibly.

'Um, hi,' she replied, before swimming quickly to her friend and pointing in my direction.

Thanks to the hot dog's minimal size, after two bites the final segment was in my mouth and I body-surfed a wave back in to the shore.

'That'll do me, Bateman,' I said as I dried myself with my towel before changing back into my shorts and T-shirt. 'Let's get out of this town that refuses to sell us alcohol.'

Even on 122nd Street, hotels and restaurants were still plentiful and it wasn't until we crossed the state line into Delaware that the world of porters and maître d's reverted to state parks and the feel of England once more. Counties of Sussex and Kent greeted us in Delaware and so did the road to Washington, D.C. where the archaic and antiquated pattern of laws was about to change. Anyone who thought that the laws I was breaking were stupid and old-fashioned simply because they had been drafted to serve a purpose which became obsolete countless numbers of years ago should be aware that our next destination, America's capital city, was home to a law which wasn't passed until after the turn of the twenty-first century.

17

Let's Go Fly a Kite

Before leaving England, amidst the anticipation and excitement generated by the press coverage, I had been warned about only one of the twenty-five laws I had intended to break; and most of the attention came from America. Ever since the September the 11th atrocities, the US authorities have been vehemently strict about what does and does not enter American airspace. In particular, without prior permission nothing is allowed to fly over the nation's capital – not even, as it turns out, a kite.

Bateman and I were only too happy to leave our downtown motel early in the morning. The previous evening Bateman had gone out to buy some cigarettes and had met some people in the street who had struck up some sort of conversation with him which was not to his liking. Upon his return to our room he had quickly secured every lock.

'I didn't think I was ever gonna get out of that alive. This is a dangerous place, mate.'

We checked out of the motel with the task ahead fresh in our mind, and stepped out of reception into a day of tremendous heat without a breath of wind. Not ideal kite-flying conditions.

What I first noticed about the city was that there were more presidential memorials and museums dedicated to celebrated Americans than you could shake a stick at. At every pedestrian crossing, we would wait patiently as hordes of tourists swept past us on a well-worn (and signposted) trail to the next monument. We were happy just to find a parking space, which we did after passing the Smithsonian Institution for a third time, quietly scared that the horrors of Oxford, Mississippi might replicate themselves in Washington. We parked on 4th Street where it crossed the Mall – an avenue of cut grass with the phallic-shaped Washington Monument at one end and the United States Capitol building over a mile away at the other. Two iconic American buildings, which I had previously only seen on the reverse of the dollar bills, were now equidistant from our car with just a turn of the head needed to capture them both. More important, the distance between the two was more than enough to run with a kite. All I needed now was to find one.

The trouble with Washington is that when the countless monuments were being built, the vast amount of materials they used seemingly prevented the building of shops and other city amenities. On the walk to the Washington Monument from the car I can only remember passing museums and an art gallery, and when we turned up towards the White House the only things which resembled a shop were the Chevy Chase Bank and a number of trolley-like stands which sold tacky souvenirs and 'I love Washington' T-shirts – and at that moment in time, I certainly didn't.

After filtering through the mass of people who stood outside the gates of the White House, waiting for the exact moment to snap their friends and family without some passer-by entering the shot, Bateman and I retraced our steps in search of a lamppost banner I had seen which advertised the city's shopping district. The Golden Triangle, just north of the White House, was made up of several streets and avenues and its slogan was more than convincing in the toy-finding department – 'The Golden Triangle: 6 hotels, 20 restaurants and 600 shops.' Surely there was a kite hiding somewhere in there.

After an hour in the Golden Triangle, all we'd found of interest was a Subway which provided us with a sandwich for lunch. By this time the extreme heat was causing my feet to sweat so much that my flip-flops were beginning to squeak with every step I took. I visited an electronics store next door in the hope that one of the employees might assist me in my search.

'Excuse me. You wouldn't know of anywhere I could buy a kite, would you?'

'A kite?' The woman almost choked on her chewing gum. I might as well have asked if I could buy a Soviet nuclear warhead. 'No, I don't know any kite shops.'

'Well, obviously I'm not looking for a kite shop. I'm sure I won't find one of them, just a place which might sell a kite.'

'No, sorry, sir. There's a guy on the corner whose job it is to find shops in the Triangle, though. He'll help you.'

The man in question stood at the end of the street and, appropriately, was dressed in gold.

'Yes, sir? May I help you?'

'I'm wondering if you know of any place that might sell a kite?'

'A kite?'

What was it with a kite? It might not be the most commonly requested item but it wasn't as bizarre or unique as the public's response suggested. Maybe buying kites was as illegal as flying them.

The man consulted his clipboard. 'I'll have to radio HQ,' he said, raising his walkie-talkie to his mouth. 'We have a gentleman requesting a kite.' The radio crackled before a voice responded: 'A kite?'

While we waited for further information, a lady who had obviously overheard my request approached us and, as always, asked Bateman and me to say a few words. Most American girls love the British accent. At the moment, however, the kite was more important and it was certainly not the time for an 'actually'. I asked her to return the favour.

'You don't know anywhere I can buy a kite, do you?'

'No.'

A similar response came from the guide when HQ finally got back in contact with him. The Golden Triangle: 6 hotels, 20 restaurants, 600 shops, 0 kites.

'Let's go back to the car and find a Wal-Mart, mate. They've always helped us out in the past. They'll have a kite, they're bound to,' I said confidently. Bateman didn't look too convinced.

A few miles out of the centre of Washington, over the Potomac River and into Virginia, we stuck to Route 1 which we were sure would take us to some sort of out-of-town shopping complex. In Target, a shop which is similar to Wal-Mart in nearly every way other than the uniform of the employees, Vladimir was the first person who didn't express disbelief at my question and led me to where he was sure he had seen such an item before.

'It was rot here,' he said, pointing at a shelf, now dominated by Barbie products.

'Hey, I don't even mind if it's a Barbie kite, mate,' I replied in desperation as Vladimir wandered off to speak to a colleague.

'No, there are no kites here, sorry.'

'Can you tell me where the nearest Wal-Mart is, please?'

'Yes, yes. Just stick to Raw One.' Raw One it was.

Several miles down 'Raw One' and with no Wal-Mart in sight, we passed another Target but thought it wiser to press on. Wal-Mart had never let us down in the past. At the next shopping complex I asked a man pushing a trolley if he knew where the department store was. Unfortunately, he couldn't speak English, so I moved on to a boy in his teens who did his best to inform me that 'it may be down there'. Strange that in the nation's capital hardly anyone spoke English. As it turned out, Wal-Mart *was* 'down there' and was actually the next building along, a hundred yards away from where we stood.

Entering the store, I ran instantly to the toy department and was greeted by a woman who, luckily, spoke perfect English.

'Excuse me, but I was wondering if you sold kites? I've been looking for one for hours.'

'We do . . .' The news almost dropped me to my knees. My search was almost at an end. '. . . just not at this time of year.' Shit.

'Right, that's it!' I shouted at Bateman.

'You giving up?' he asked.

I must admit, I had thought about it, but breaking this law would mean four successes on the trot, an accomplishment I had never achieved before.

'No. I'm going to make one.'

'What?'

'Come on, it can't be that difficult. I made one at

school once. It didn't fly, but I'm older and wiser now. I'm sure I can do better this time. What stuff do I need? It's all here.'

Although it didn't seem likely when they were scanned by Sue on the checkout, the very economical $3.74's worth of items which my basket contained were all I needed to construct the perfect kite.

Now, children, this is what you'll need to make your very own kite to fly in a shopping centre car park just outside Washington, D.C.:

- A packet of 10 bin liners
- A carton of 75 drinking straws
- Some sticky tape
- The remaining line of catgut you used when you tried to catch a fish with a lasso in Tennessee
- And a pair of scissors (but do ask an adult to do the cutting)

1 Return to your car and place a bin liner on the boot of vehicle. Unfortunately, the wind which has by now picked up will create bad kite-preparation conditions but will no doubt aid the eventual flight attempt once you return to the city.

2 To the best of your ability, cut a square shape out of the bin liner (it's best if you cut down along the seams of the liner which will then open out in such a shape).

3 As your assistant holds the kite flat, count how

many straws will be needed to line it in an X fashion across its reverse.

4 By squeezing the end of the straws, you can feed them into each other to make one big straw which will hopefully reach from the top corner to the bottom one. Repeat procedure for the two remaining corners.

5 Once the straw frames have been made, fasten them down with sticky tape. This will now act as the kite's support and will stop it from simply folding under pressure from the wind.

6 Tell any passers-by who may have heard you talk in your English accent and want you to say a few words that 'the only thing that springs to mind is: I'd love to but can't you see I'm busy making a kite?'

7 Cut four equal lengths of catgut (a good measurement is the distance between Bateman's foot and the bridge of his nose).

8 Fasten the ends of the four lengths of catgut to each of the corners of the bin liner with sticky tape and collect the four other ends in your right or left hand.

9 Return to Washington, D.C. feeling ever so slightly proud of your accomplishment.

Upon our return to the city, through the rush-hour traffic we seemed to be plagued by no matter how well we prepared to avoid it, we parked just opposite the Mall and I made my way onto the freshly cut grass, kite in hand. The wind, which had not helped during the making of the kite, had suddenly disappeared now that its presence was an absolute necessity. Even the dozens of American flags which surrounded the Washington Monument half a mile away were drooping or motionless. What was worse was the discovery that somewhere on the journey from Wal-Mart to the Mall the kite had somehow lost a piece of catgut and now had only three lines.

'Run with it!' Bateman shouted from where he stood with camera in hand, ready to capture the moment.

I began to run towards the monument, but the heat and my lack of fitness quickly tired me out. I needn't have even tried. The kite simply dragged along the ground, never lifting more than a couple of feet off the ground and getting some of its straw framework pulled loose in the process.

10 Ensure that your kite isn't a badly made piece of crap.

Undeterred, I got my second wind. With my hopes of achieving take-off picking up with the early evening breeze, I went back to the car to make some final adjustments to the straws, and returned to the grass for a final attempt. As I walked down to the centre of the Mall, I felt a slight stirring on my neck and instantly sprang into action, unfolding the kite and throwing it into the air, where it was caught and whisked aloft by the only gust of wind to hit the Mall that day. Clutching the three remaining strings with my arms at full stretch, I thought the kite – which must have soared to at least fifteen feet – looked as majestic in its upward surge as an eagle in full flight ... well, as much as a bin liner with sixteen coloured straws attached can resemble a bird of prey. Although Bateman didn't capture the brief moment on camera, and instead photographed only the before and after of the flight, at least the law was broken and four successes in a row had been achieved. I cast my mind back to the moment when I sat in a Los Angeles hotel room peeling an orange in a desperate, yet easy, attempt to begin the spree, and four was a feat of which I could only dream. Yet here I was, in searing heat with a set of complete strangers staring at me and my bin liner. I felt ever so slightly heroic, and stood as proudly as the monument at the end of the Mall.

'To the car, Bateman. Our work here is complete.'

Surrounded yet again by rush-hour traffic, we managed to find Interstate 270 which would carry us north towards our next destination. We pulled off at a motel in a small town called Hagerstown, which lies just south of Maryland's border with Pennsylvania; it was time to check how well Bateman and 'Lisa's' long-distance relationship was blossoming. Judging from what Bateman had written it was coming on in leaps and bounds – so well in fact that Bateman had asked what 'Lisa' was doing the week after I was due to fly home. As luck would have it, 'Lisa' was off that week and, if Bateman wanted to, he was free to spend it in sunny Indianapolis with her and frequent the local nightspots.

Bateman's email wasn't the only fresh message in my inbox that evening and the second was, amazingly, even more of a joy to read. It was from a gentleman by the name of Kevin Harvey who represented the picture desk of the *Metro* newspaper in London. He explained that he was very interested in my 'unique crime spree' and, more surprisingly, my 'proposed underwater bike ride along the River Thames'. What on earth was he talking about? When I had replied to Kevin, querying the origin of the biking rumour, I passed the laptop back over to Bateman. He didn't seem too bothered when I told him about the bizarre message I had just received. Mind you, he had just found out he could stay in Indianapolis for free.

For the first time on the holiday, I wasn't thinking about the next law I was planning on breaking, but instead about what I might do when I returned home. Riding a bike underwater along the River Thames? What a bloody good idea.

18

Suite Dreams

Our motel in Hagerstown must be some way out from the centre of the town, I deduced from the lack of houses to be seen from the car park. What was situated near the motel, though, and was the subject of half the advertising brochures in the shelving racks near the reception desk, was an outlet mall: Prime Outlets of Hagerstown. Having never been to an outlet mall before and knowing that at the very least it gave us an ideal chance to buy some cheap clothes and presents for friends and family back home, we decided to leave travelling to Pittsburgh for later on in the morning and concentrated on visiting the mall.

Since Hagerstown was just a subdued outpost on Maryland's border with Pennsylvania, I was surprised when we had to wait for over five minutes just to join the queue of traffic heading down from our motel. When the congestion eased and we began to inch our way under the interstate and towards the mall, there were no signs to suggest there had been any kind of accident or clues as to why the traffic had come to a standstill for such a prolonged amount of time. As we edged forward we noticed a petrol station with an unusual number of motorcycles filling up – four using the pumps, and another five waiting in line. A little further on, as we waited to pull in to our goal, we heard an unremitting sound of approaching thunder. The vehicle in front of us had left a gap to allow crossing traffic to enter the mall, and the deafening roar was explained as dozens of motorcycles suddenly fed through the break and down into the mall.

Our eventual arrival in the mall's car park was one of the most surreal experiences of my life. The motorbikes we had first seen in the petrol station and the ones we had waited patiently for as they crossed our path minutes later were just a handful of the hundreds and hundreds already parked up, and more were filtering through from all directions. Harley-Davidsons, Yamahas, Suzukis and Hondas were all there, along with the biggest collections of moustaches and bandannas ever seen in one place. Thinking it was either some sort of world record attempt or a Hell's Angels' reunion, Bateman and I stood reverently in the doorways of our car, and the overall roar of the engines grew in power and volume as more and more bikes joined the procession. The bikers who had arrived already gave each other pats on the back and enjoyed some food or drink at the trailers which had been laid on for their arrival, while a loudspeaker stand waited to be used to let us all in on the secret.

As we locked the car and made our way towards the horde of bikers, hoping to find out why they had convened in such a great number and in such an insignificant town, we passed what Bateman described as 'the coolest bike of the lot'.

Standing apart from the rest so that it could be admired by all was a Harley-Davidson with perfectly burnished engine and valves which gleamed beneath the stars and stripes of the American flag emblazoned on its body. Whatever the reason for this un-precedented crowd of bikers – and new arrivals were still flooding in – this particular bike seemed to embody it.

The outlet mall was laid out like a little town, similar to a model a child might make out of building blocks except that the grouping of shops had only pedestrian thoroughfares and was surrounded by what would normally be considered an enormous car park, but was now at bursting point due to the motor-bike manifestation.

In the Adidas outlet store I purchased a pair of trousers and a shirt (a bargain at thirty dollars) and began talking to the sales assistant about the most pressing matter on my mind.

'Why are there about a thousand motorbikes parked in the car park?'

She peered through the automatic doors as if to check I wasn't just making it up. 'I'm not really sure. I haven't heard anything about it, anyway,' she replied. 'I love your accents! What you doing over here?'

Throughout the trip, that had been the most difficult question to answer. If I was in a pub or a place where I was settled and in the mood for a string of questions related to the origin and highlights of my journey, I would always give a truthful response. In small-talk situations I would merely suggest that I was just travelling around the country, but if I divulged this information to any small-town resident I would always fall prey to the same reaction. They would always be shocked that a tourist had chosen their town to visit, and wonder why I had pencilled that particular place into my holiday itinerary as a must-see location.

'Oh, I'm just travelling around America,' I replied coyly.

'Why the hell did you come here?' No difference here then.

Queuing at one of Prime Outlet's food courts, where nearly every fast food chain is represented, I happened to catch a glimpse of the back of a man's T-shirt which seemed to suggest the reason for the motorcyclists' grand gathering. As his ponytail waved from side to side and revealed more of the text, it appeared that Hagerstown was a major stop-off point in the 5th Annual 9/11 Commemorative Ride and that this year's course was taking them from North

Carolina to Philadelphia and would finish in New York City in a couple of days' time. As I took a final glance at the T-shirt before joining Bateman at one of the food court's tables, a thought suddenly occurred to me. Quite apart from its being August, which straight away seemed an odd month to commemorate something that happened in September, like wearing poppies in March or waiting until June to chuck an effigy of Guy Fawkes on a pile of pallets and worthless wood before igniting it all, it struck me as very peculiar that in Hagerstown in August 2005 the 5th Annual 9/11 Commemorative Ride was taking place before even four years had passed since the Twin Towers disaster.

An hour after arriving we were set to leave and make our way to Pittsburgh – at the same time as the bikers were departing for Philadelphia it seemed. Fifteen minutes of revving engines, swarms and gusts of exhaust fumes, and even a news helicopter circling and monitoring their every move, and all but a few of the bikers had vanished, leaving the car park forlorn and godforsaken. It was time to head north into Pennsylvania where the day was only going to become stranger, as I hoped to wake up the following morning on top of a fridge.

Without any overwhelming need to rush, and with me being a cheapskate, we decided to stay off the toll interstate roads which are common in the built-up areas of the east and remained just shy of the border before turning north towards Pittsburgh through impressively named towns such as Accident, Laboratory and, my personal favourite, Eighty Four. *Strange American Town Names* and *America's Greatest Roundabouts* – two fascinating TV series in their infancy that are just waiting to be commissioned. BBC, take note – if you don't snap them up, a cable channel with fewer than a thousand viewers will certainly snatch them from under your noses.

It's always nice to enter a new state, especially one I've never visited before. By this stage, there was a comfortable routine: over the border and into the inevitable rest area with connecting tourist information centres to find a new motel coupon book. Pennsylvania's was exceptionally valuable and rewarding. It would help me find a hotel within the city limits of Pittsburgh which could be guaranteed to have a refrigerator.

As well as being home to America's original capital city of Philadelphia, the 'Keystone State' also harbours two of the greatest laws I had come across, though admittedly the one I had chosen to break was a challenge I wasn't particularly looking forward to. In Pennsylvania, a law which must have been drafted at the same time as the introduction of the automobile stresses that if a horse approaches a motorist he or she must cover the car in a blanket or canvas which blends into its surroundings and allow the horse to pass. If the horse still appears skittish, the motorist must take his car apart piece by piece and hide it under the nearest tree. In order to break that law I would simply have to ignore all of the above and leave my car intact in the presence of a horse, something I was sure every Pennsylvanian does anyway. However, I was pretty certain that only a handful of people had slept on top of a refrigerator, and for that reason alone I was heading for Pittsburgh.

Only four miles from the centre of the city, our motel seemed to be light years away from any sort of civilization. With not even a single branch of any fast food chain on the horizon, and only a petrol station and equally bleak accommodations nearby, we randomly chose a motel at the top of a barren hill whose most distinguishing attribute was a plentiful supply of roadkill lying by the barriers at the bottom. Normally a motel coupon's lowered price would be accepted on any day of the week except Fridays and Saturdays, but going by the empty look of the car park outside the Comfort Inn we were hoping that this, one of the few motels with a refrigerator, would look on our weekend stay with a kindly eye.

Danielle, the receptionist, was quietly watching the Golf Channel when I entered with coupon book in hand.

'Sorry to interrupt you, but I was wondering how much a double room for this evening would be?' I asked. 'I've got a coupon.'

'Sorry,' she said. 'It really only counts for Sunday through Thursdays. A room will be eighty dollars.'

'Eighty dollars?' I asked, holding out the coupon which discounted the rate to sixty dollars on other days of the week. 'Can't you do me some sort of Englishman deal?'

Danielle looked at the screen of her computer and a smile came to her face. 'Seeing I like your accents, how about a room for eighty dollars and I'll give you a room with a Jacuzzi? Normally priced at a hundred twenty?'

'Yeah, sure,' we replied. 'Has it got a fridge?' I added.

'A refrigerator, you mean?'

'Well, it's just easier to say fridge. That's what we call it back home.'

'All of our rooms have . . . um . . . fridges.' Danielle came out from behind the desk. 'Follow me; I'll show you one of our Jacuzzi rooms.'

Just round the corner stood the door to room 112, the Jacuzzi suite we were to be shown. Up to now we'd stayed in our fair share of dismal hovels but our own Jacuzzi room was going to make up for the lot of them (even if I was to spend the night in the most uncomfortable of places).

'Here it is, boys. King-size bed, desk, Jacuzzi and . . .' she looked around, puzzled, '. . . there doesn't seem to be a pull-out bed, just an armchair and footrest.' I didn't mind. The room had a decent-sized fridge and that's all I cared about.

'That doesn't matter. We'll take this room,' I said.

'I can find a room with a pull-out if you want but it won't have a Jacuzzi.'

'I don't mind lying on the armchair,' Bateman volunteered.

'You'll be on the bed, won't you, obviously,' I said, tilting my head and raising my eyebrows to remind Bateman of just why we were here but possibly giving Danielle a completely different impression.

'Oh. OK then,' she said, stepping away from the Jacuzzi and almost running out of the door and back to her desk.

The armchair, footrest and fridge (once it had been disconnected from the wall, dragged across the floor and laid on its side) were of almost uniform height and were pieced together to form my 'bed'. Although the fridge was an inch or so higher than the chair and footrest, which made up the head and tail ends, once a blanket had been placed over the lot, it didn't look too uncomfortable and I was positive I had slept in more awkward positions after a night of heavy drinking than on top of a fridge. In a phone box and under a car were two that instantly sprang to mind.

'Right, Bateman. You're gonna like this. The only way I'm going to be able to sleep on this fridge tonight is by getting so hammered I won't care where I sleep. Pub?'

You don't have to ask Bateman twice.

Unfortunately for us, the pub was at the bottom of the very steep hill, on top of which the motel was situated, and walking down the main road seemed the only way of getting to it. Walking outside the road's metal barrier was virtually impossible as it meant wading through long shoots of grass which were probably filled with venomous creatures, so we elected to wander down the side of the road facing the cars that came hurtling round the corner and forced us back into the barrier. If it was this terrifying when I was sober, there was no guarantee I would even make it back to the motel by the time I was drunk enough to face the prospect of walking back up the hill to sleep on a refrigerator.

In the pub we both delved into our first pint as I quickly made doubly sure, before it was too late, that the law prohibited sleeping *on* a refrigerator and not *in* one.

Although my memory of the night in question is very hazy, three things definitely happened, all of which I can recollect clearly. Bateman and I both enjoyed chicken Caesar salads which were advertised as 'salads as big as your heads'. Secondly, I must have been drunker than I have ever been in my life as, apart from the fact that I definitely left the pub before Bateman, I have no memory whatsoever of my pre-sumably life-threatening walk back up to our motel. The next time I saw Bateman was when he woke me in the middle of the night in the most spectacular of fashions. This I remember well.

'Bateman?' I said, lifting my face off my drool-drenched pillow. 'Why are you in the Jacuzzi with all your clothes on? You're bloody soaking.'

'I dunno. I must have fallen in,' he sniggered.

'Is that the camera you have in your hand? It bloody

is. Don't drop it in the water. Why the hell have you got it anyway?'

'I was taking a picture of you. I've taken two actually. You should be happy I remembered. I had to go to the car to get the camera.'

'But why?'

'I thought you'd want a picture of you passed out on a fridge.'

I'd passed out on the fridge? Excellent.

19

Fore-bidden

August the 21st was the only day of the holiday I wasn't looking forward to, and when it finally arrived I felt a wave of homesickness. It was inevitable, and I'd expected it ever since I had first realized I would be in America on that particular Sunday. It wasn't so much that I missed my family, friends or life back in England; it was for the simple reason that 21 August is when the residents of my home village celebrate Portreath Harbour Fun Day. At eight o'clock in the morning I knew that it was one in the afternoon back home and people were already well on the way to securing their Monday hangovers. Although it is primarily aimed at children and tourists, the local ideology is that the occasion should be treated as an all-day drinking marathon, and my brother and our friends have crammed into my tiny back garden, drinks in hand, from noon onwards since I could first hold a pint glass. Local fishermen offer free boat trips round the bay, the 'greasy pole' is positioned in the centre of the harbour bestridden by children who swing pillows wildly at each other in an attempt to knock their opponent into the water below, and the entrants in the raft race have to endure a pelting with eggs and flour thrown by the spectators who stand above using the competitors as target practice. All in all, Harbour Fun Day is loved and despised in equal measures by the locals, and I was saddened to be so far from an event I haven't missed since I drank three bottles of red wine in forty-five minutes in 1998 and passed out at two in the afternoon, not waking up until the following day.

To compensate for our absence on the special day, it was decided that we should be near water, and even if we didn't drink the very least we would do was enjoy ourselves, take a day off and do something different. It was for this reason that I was awake early in our motel less than five miles from Niagara Falls where our very own unique Harbour Fun Day would be spent.

When I'd had a shower and forced Bateman to do the same, I picked up the room's television remote control and watched a live news report from New York on FOX News. It looked as if the bikers' 5th Annual 9/11 Commemorative Ride had come to a successful finale in the Big Apple and the featured bike, next to which the reporter stood, was the stars and stripes Harley-Davidson I had seen in Hagerstown two days before.

Strangely, there are three Niagara Falls and only one of them is a waterfall. The town of Niagara Falls, New York, a rather unimpressive place of cheap tourist attractions and casinos, sits across the Niagara River from the Canadian town of Niagara Falls, Ontario, which certainly looked as if it had cashed in on the American half-assed attempt to lure tourists to their side with million-dollar hotels and observation towers standing amongst perfectly kept gardens and pruned hedges.

As we parked outside a church which flew the English flag on top of its tower, we made our way towards the falls and en route continued our new game – our own quiz on events in America.

'OK, then,' I began, 'in what town did you go missing when you ended up with that tart?'

'I can't remember. I was pissed.'

'It was Grand Island. What country did Joye's mother come from?'

'I dunno.'

'Honduras. You're not very good at this, are you, Bateman? What was the name of—'

Bateman interrupted me. I could feel he was beginning to grow a little annoyed. 'OK then. What was the name of the bird who met us at the Indianapolis radio station?'

I took a few steps back so Bateman couldn't see the

smile which was fast growing on my face. 'Um . . . it wasn't Lisa, was it?'

'Yeah,' Bateman droned.

'How did you remember that?' I asked.

Bateman turned to me and prepared for the biggest gloat of his life. 'I've been emailing her since we left and I might go over there and see her when you fly home and before I go to Miami.'

'Really? Well, I wouldn't bother if I were you, mate.'

'Why not? She seems really up for it.'

'Yeah, but Lisa of indianaradiogirl@hotmail.com is me, mate.'

Bateman paused for a second or two before summing up an opinion on the matter. 'Prick.'

'Hey, you should be thankful; I could have made you fly all the way to Indianapolis, you know.'

'Yeah, and if you did, I would have beaten the shit out of you.'

Niagara Falls is made up of three waterfalls of which the American Falls and the Horseshoe Falls are the better known. From where we had parked, the gentle flow of the river and the peaceful woodland surroundings would never have you believe that the docile mood of the water is just seconds away from a 188-foot drop into a powerful and dramatic explosion which shrouds the descent in a permanent cloud of spray that rises higher than the top of the falls.

Horseshoe Falls is, by far, the most impressive of the three, probably because 90 per cent of Niagara's water is driven over its precipice. Below, tour boats take tourists as close as they possibly can to the foot of the falls, and position them on the very brink of certain destruction where the conditions must be similar to a wind and rain-swept gale of epic proportions. Like most tourist locations, the viewing position for the Horseshoe Falls is crammed with a cultural mix of people in which it seems every creed, colour and religion is represented. From there, they can witness the magnificent sight of 600,000 gallons of water plunging every second from the 2,200-foot-long rim of the falls like an azure tablecloth draped over jagged rocks.

To gain a better view of the Horseshoe Falls, Bateman and I made our way over the Rainbow Bridge and into Canada. From the other side of the river, the Canadians get the best views and it comes as no surprise that hotels and observation towers make up the front line of Canadian buildings. Here, the true beauty of both the American and the Horseshoe Falls can be viewed in their entirety; on the American side of the river it feels more like you're standing on their shoulders.

At over two hundred feet above the Horseshoe Falls and more than half a mile away from the base, I could still feel the spray from the falling water. Returning to the bridge, we joined the back of the queue for US immigration. Entering Canada was simple. Proffer your passport and answer the usual questions, and the process takes no longer than a minute. Re-entering the US is an entirely different experience. For starters it costs fifty cents. As we waited in line, not a single queuing person was being seen by officials and we could hear an immigration officer shouting at someone about a pram. A family sitting by us was looking terribly anxious and I wondered if they were the cause of the temporary break in the formalities. As in all immigration experiences, when we were finally seen we were eyed with suspicion and distrust and greeted in the usual obnoxious and unwelcoming way.

'And when did you last travel in the United States, sir?'

'About fifteen minutes ago. I only popped over to see the falls.'

'What have you brought with you?'

'Just my wallet and passport. I had a hot dog but I've eaten that.'

With no further line of questioning available to him, he allowed me into the United States, calling the next person in line to come forward to brighten their day. Stepping out of the office and back onto American soil, I calculated that we had spent more time in the immigration office than we had at the falls. Bateman reckoned that as he had now been to Canada, this marked the beginning of his second trip to America.

With Harbour Fun Day over for another year, it was time to concentrate on the law-breaking and law number twenty – hopefully the fourteenth success and a record sixth in a row. Approximately three hundred miles south-east of Niagara lay Albany, the capital of New York State, where it was illegal to play golf in the streets of the city.

I've been known to play a round or two in my time and my dad plays religiously. To be honest, I'm not very good, and I don't see the point in traipsing round a large field looking for a ball in wintry conditions. It's still a surprise to me how the game caught on in the first place and why people took a Scotsman seriously when he suggested that trying to get a small ball into a slightly larger hole four hundred yards away was a good idea. What was more, there would be bits of sand and water as obstacles in the way. They must have thought he was mental.

Not wanting to spend more than ten or so dollars on any serious stuff, I went for the rather less sporting option of visiting Toys 'Я' Us and purchasing the originally named 'Beginners Golf Set'. Luckily for me, the quality kit not only included a club and several balls but even came complete with its own holes (little rings) and flags at which to aim.

Albany's state capitol building was unlike any of the others we had seen. In Salt Lake City, Indianapolis and elsewhere, you basically find a scaled-down model of the United States Capitol building in Washington – Greek-style stone pillars with a domed roof. Albany's is as exuberant as the Casino de Monte Carlo and is similar in appearance to an alpine Bavarian castle, surrounded by corporate buildings and museums in what appears to be a very affluent area of the city. Lining State Street, where all of these buildings are placed, was the largest collection of food vending vans I have ever seen in my life – and I've been to more than my fair share of car boot sales and fairgrounds. Twelve vans in all, each with a raised metal awning, fought against the competition and had something very different to offer. The standard breakfast roll and hot dog van vied with Greek, Italian and Turkish versions, plus some other cuisines I couldn't pronounce, never mind identify. They all tried to lure the many customers who had flocked out of nearby office buildings to spend their lunch breaks in the park. It seemed the ideal location in which to begin making a country club golf course – albeit only one hole.

The following description of the hole is best read in the style of Peter Alliss commentating at the beginning of the British Open. Listen as he talks you through this tricky ninety-yarder. The raised edge of the sidewalk and the steps of the Albany Board of Education building provide the ideal location for the tee of this, a tricky ninety-odd-yard par six at the Downtown Albany Country Club. From here, the golfer will attempt to avoid traffic and pedestrians and can feel proud of himself if his ball lands on the opposite sidewalk and isn't hooked deep into the construction yard to the left of the fairway. A slice to the right will require luck to squeeze between the curry and kebab vans which are targets worth evading. Across the road, from the foot of the capitol the hole follows the path of a nasty dogleg where the ball should be kept to the right at all times, avoiding the building's fountain which supplies the most picturesque of water hazards. From here, the choice to go for the green is an awfully tempting one but very often players have fallen short, leaving them with a difficult shot: lofting the ball over the park bench and onto the green above. Two simple putts, made more taxing by the absence of a putter in the set, should conclude the hole, the round and the breaking of the law. Time to tee off.

Bateman made a grand caddy even if he didn't have any clubs to carry. My first shot (with a slight hook) saw the ball drift past the construction site and – amazingly – to the foot of the capitol's steps. After that rather impressive first shot, I definitely had to avoid the fountain or Bateman would invoke the 'play it from where it lies' rule for a cheap laugh.

As the club lifted into the air, I was distracted by people both behind and in front of where I stood.

'Hang on,' Bateman called. 'People coming down the steps.'

Some dignitaries walking down the steps from the capitol examined me curiously as they made their way across the road and away from the vans – they were obviously important enough to turn their noses up at a bacon bap. After that, we were further delayed while two security guards crossed the 'fairway', staring vacantly at me but not batting a single eyelid between them.

Hoisted high into the air, the ball dropped short and

to the right of the fountain, which meant just a six or seven-foot walk forward for shot number three. The third shot, struck with precision, was meant for the green but lacked sufficient pace to clear the park bench. Unluckily, the ball was left directly in front of the bench – which was by this time in use by a man who had sat down to eat his lunch. If my sand wedge couldn't clear his sandwich as well as him I was in trouble – and not only from the man himself for interrupting his meal. After a pleasing start, I would almost certainly finish the round over par if this shot failed to make it onto the green for a two-putt finish.

Throwing caution to the wind, I hit the bottom of the ball firmly, clearing bench, gentleman and green quite convincingly. A quick and safe approach shot back to the green left me with a single putt for par – a shot that would have been successfully taken care of if a putter had been up for selection. Without it, I hopelessly chipped the ball over the hole before tapping it in for seven. One over par.

The day's result wasn't too disheartening. So what if I had ended the round with a seven and not the required six? All I cared about was that law twenty had been a success and left us with fourteen victories overall. Picking my ball out of the hole and waving to the crowd, who didn't seem to care less what I was doing, I packed the kit back into the car and wondered what to do next. The nineteenth hole (or in this case the second) was the preferred option for celebration, and I didn't need a great deal of persuading by

Bateman to settle for post-round potations at Hooters.

In the beautiful surroundings that only Hooters girls can provide, and with my two-week-old goatee now looking pretty impressive, albeit a slightly disturbing shade of ginger, Bateman and I toasted the next and final stage of our journey. The following day we would set off on our way north through New England, a region in which we would remain until we travelled to New Jersey for the final law.

The prospect of seeing New England was exciting enough, but I was really looking forward to the next law for one simple reason – it would end with the removal of my goatee, which I was just itching to shave off.

20

The Boston Goatee Party

I was counting this as my sixth visit to America, though going by Bateman's Niagara Falls theory it was at least my twelfth. On every visit I'd made to the States, for one reason or another, I had missed New England out completely. It's one of the only places in the country I had always wanted to visit and yet had never made a conscious effort to get to. Even though the book of laws had not thought too highly of it and only had three good laws to cover two of the six states that make up the region, I was glad that fate had finally delivered me to an area of the country I hadn't seen before.

Just as I'd imagined, New England was beautiful, and New Hampshire's expanse of trees and woodland surrounding every road we joined, flowing in an undulating wave of luscious green to the blue sky of the horizon, was ample proof of that. The towns through which the road weaved felt homely and familiar and I was sure I had seen them in American family movies where everyone knows everyone else and the local postmaster is also the town mayor. It was in a town like this, where we pulled over to refuel, that I realized just how visually stunning this part of eastern America is. Below me a river ran gently under a bridge connecting the eastern and western parts of the town, which stood below a mass of trees that looked as if it could easily swallow every building. When I paid for the fuel, I noticed that the garage sold salt and vinegar flavour crisps, which I had failed to find in any other state until now.

Instead of simply taking the interstate directly to Boston, we decided to make our way to the coast and work our way down the Atlantic seaboard before entering Massachusetts. Just south of Portsmouth and less than twenty miles from the border with Massachusetts stood the town of Rye, a little village just north of the larger settlement of Hampton. Here, Bateman and I decided to spend a bit of time on the beach as it was the first time I had seen the ocean since leaving Los Angeles and the first time I'd seen the Atlantic since I had left home.

Rye Beach reminded us of how time at the seaside ought to be spent. Children dug holes on the beach, using the upturned piles of sand as makeshift forts and castles; there was no pier, no amusement arcade, a half-mile walk to the nearest refreshment providers;

and the only sources of entertainment were the sea and sand themselves.

After a surprisingly cold swim, probably due to the fact that the closest land masses to Rye are Greenland and Canada, I returned to our spot on the beach, I could hear an ice-cream van play 'The Entertainer' over and over again until all the children had purchased their frozen desserts and the van departed, only to turn down the next road to the beach and repeat the routine. Then the van appeared no more than twenty yards from me. I waited for the dulcet tones of 'Greensleeves' or a stirring rendition of 'Oh When the Saints' to resonate around the beach. Even 'The Birdie Song' would have been an improvement on a tune I'd heard dozens of times already. As soon as the van parked up and opened its awning to serve the first of its customers, Scott Joplin's ragtime classic hit my ears and I began to feel a deep sense of loathing for snooker and Dennis Taylor's upside-down glasses. It didn't play the full version, or even the shortened version, but the first thirty seconds over and over again. I counted that, after the tune had finished, it was repeated no fewer than thirty-one times before the awning was finally retracted and the van moved on. Thank God.

'If I hear that tune one more pissing time, Bateman, there's gonna be big trouble in little Rye. How annoying is it?' I asked, not sure of what my 'Entertainer' encore action was going to be.

'When we gonna go anyway? I get bored just lying

on the beach,' he said, just as the van appeared fifty yards further down the beach at an opening I hadn't realized was there.

'Now. Quickly.'

Technically, as soon as I entered Massachusetts sporting my goatee I had broken the law, but I felt that simply crossing the border wasn't good enough and I wanted to have my picture taken somewhere memorable and somewhere that oozes Massachusetts. Like the beer in the bucket in St Louis, the goatee had to be taken somewhere special: a place where it knew it was breaking the law and that was visually palpably in Massachusetts.

Ruling out Cape Cod as 'too far away' (me) and 'too boring' (Bateman), we decided we would find a decent motel on the outskirts of Boston and explore the city the following day, treating the goatee to a nice day out. The motel we eventually found met at least one of my two criteria – it was on the outskirts.

After a few days without a drop of alcohol I knew it was only a matter of time before Bateman demanded we went drinking, and as he rose from his bed and reached for his shoes I was pretty sure what he was about to suggest.

We settled for a pub just down the road from our motel, simply because it had free snacks at the bar and the Boston Red Sox game was being shown on the big screen. On previous trips I would have stayed clear of any establishment airing a baseball game but after several weeks in the country I had developed a liking for their version of English rounders and, what's more, Boston's team were the current champions of the World Series.

After several pints, Bateman and I were refused service on the grounds that we had had too much to drink already. I would have understood if there had been evidence to back up her claim but we were sitting quietly in our chairs, weren't abusive in any way, could hold a civilized conversation – which in this case was: 'Why can't we have another drink?' – and came from a country where if you had managed to drag yourself to the bar under your own steam and could pronounce your order reasonably well, that was testament enough that you could still manage another drink or two.

'OK,' said Bateman to the bar lady, 'we'll just go to another bar then.' So we did. To the one next door.

Unlike the previous place, our new Boston local was dimly lit, showed the baseball on a tiny screen in the corner, and was full of people who all seemed depressed about something or other. I loved it. This was like a British pub, and if we could manage to drag ourselves to the bar it would be drinks galore. Bateman, obviously still annoyed after our experience in the first bar, took it upon himself to upgrade our level of drinking and ordered a couple of whiskies. After a few rounds of those I wouldn't have blamed the barman for asking us to leave and I turned my attention to a games machine in the corner of the bar which involved hitting a penguin with a baseball bat.

As always, once I had reached level two a gentleman appeared over my shoulder to offer his opinion on how the game should be played.

'You should play the poker game, buddy,' he said.

'Nah, I'm quite happy hitting this penguin into the middle of next week, thanks.'

The man was one of those guys no one likes: the kind of guy who offers you advice on gambling machines or dictates the pace at which you should hit your next shot to gain the perfect position for your next shot at the pool table. The man turned out to be called Eric; Bateman had met him earlier and he was now offering us a lift to a nearby club.

'Come on, Rich. He's parked outside,' Bateman said, standing in the doorway of the bar. There was only one reason why I went.

I don't think it was the fact that I was drunk or that I had an overwhelming desire to go to the club, but it was the second time on the holiday that I accepted a lift with a complete stranger whose car was most definitely red. I wasn't going to be cowed by Brenda's crank predictions. Bad things would happen? As far as I was concerned, they were happening already.

The club, over two miles away from the bar, was called Ups 'n' Downs and from what I can remember our arrival doubled the total occupancy, probably owing to the fact that it was a Tuesday evening and the club was in the middle of nowhere. I'm not sure how much earlier I left than Eric and Bateman but it must have been the exact amount of time it took for me to walk back to the motel as I arrived there just as they pulled up in Eric's car.

'Thanks for a good night, Luke,' Eric said as Bateman stood by the wing of the car holding the door wide open. 'I'm off back to Connecticut now, buddy.'

Bateman, by now in a horribly drunken state, fell back into the front passenger seat and slammed the door. 'I'm going too.'

After I had explained several times to Bateman that Connecticut was a completely different state and not a bigger and better nightclub further down the road, he reluctantly got out again. Eric locked the door so Bateman couldn't change his mind, and sped off. By now Bateman had noticed that there appeared to be some kind of party in progress in one of the rooms on the motel's ground floor. Asking if he wanted to come back with me to our room to pre-empt any kind of trouble he might get into, and receiving a flat-out negative reply, I returned to the room and closed the door, then peeped through the window where I could see Bateman swaying outside, talking to a few of the party guests who stood in the doorway, neither inviting him in nor asking him to leave. As I stripped down to my boxer shorts and collapsed into bed I knew it was only a matter of time before Bateman returned to the room.

In fact, it was a good hour or so before he did ... under the supervision of the Boston police. I was dressed in just boxer shorts and a T-shirt, my goatee on full display. Surely I was for it.

'Take him in and keep him here or we'll be back,' said the cop who held a shoeless Bateman.

'OK, officer. I will,' I replied as the cop and his partner began to walk away down the steps. Then they stopped.

'Just one more thing,' the officer said, turning to face me. 'Have a nice night, sir.'

Bateman, who couldn't remember any of this the following morning, said I must have dreamed the entire thing. Why he thought I would dream about a drunken Bateman was beyond me, but his suspicions were silenced when we found his shoes outside.

Boston, as I was told by the many Americans I had met en route, was a city I would love. 'They're like you' and 'they talk like you there' were generally the main reasons given. In reality Boston was a joy of a town and is one of that rare subsection of American cities – those that were built before the invention and introduction of the car. Until 1755 it was the biggest town in America and even now walking around the narrow streets gives a fascinating insight into America's beginnings. Beginnings which are even better explored with a small goatee on your face.

Obviously, a city steeped in history and culture cannot be evaluated simply on those merits alone. Oh, no. In my eyes, it must, of course, have pleasant tramps. Put to the test, Boston emerged faultless when

I told one beggar I had no spare change, to which he replied, 'That's OK. God bless you, man.' St Louis had finally been relegated to the lower leagues.

There were only two things Bateman wanted to do in Boston and, surprisingly, neither of them involved Hooters. Instead, Bateman wanted to visit the bar in which the opening credits to the sitcom *Cheers* were set and, even more alarmingly, wanted to get a tattoo.

'A tattoo? Why do you want to get a tattoo?' I asked. Bateman's answer was one I couldn't argue with.

'Because I'm in the mood.'

Not quite sure what kind of 'mood' someone has to be in to have his skin painfully and permanently painted, I was happy if I could just show my goatee a good time.

'Right. We'll go to the *Cheers* bar first though, yeah?'

What I didn't know about Boston was that there are two *Cheers* bars. One was the original which features in the opening credits of the television series and the other was created after the success of the sitcom and made to look exactly the way it does in the programme. Aware of how very few episodes I'd actually seen of *Cheers* and how little I would notice any imperfections in the bar's appearance, we both opted for the original as the perfect place for the goatee to enjoy its crowning moment.

The *Cheers* bar looked exactly like I imagined (as it would, I suppose), and a Dutch couple were already outside snapping pictures of each other under the yellow domed awnings and the *Cheers* sign, est. 1895, which shook gently in the wind. Downstairs in the bar I was sadly disappointed. It wasn't because the bar was littered with the obligatory *Cheers* paraphernalia, or because the drinks were quite highly priced. It was simply because nobody knew my name. Even Bateman, who was still showing mental repercussions from the previous night, might have struggled to remember. After a quick pint which, and I quote, Bateman had to 'battle through', we purchased two souvenir pint glasses and made our way to the local information hut where Bateman could enquire where he might have a tattoo done. In a Boston Information Center Bateman approached the desk and asked where he could get a tattoo similar to George Clooney's in *From Dusk Till Dawn*.

With only the training and knowledge of an untattooed Boston information guide to call on, his victim did what anyone else would have done: asked the guide next to her, who did have some body art, where he'd had his done.

After double-checking its position on the map, the clerk sent us in the direction of the city's excellent subway system to take a train from the centre of Boston across the Charles River and into Cambridge, where Harvard University's campus is located. Only a street away from where seven US presidents, fifty Nobel Prize winners, and countless political leaders, poets and writers had graduated from one of the most illustrious universities in the world, Bateman simply wanted to get his skin painted. Unfortunately for him, the tattooist was fully booked and the design Bateman had requested would have taken over three hours to perform.

Slightly downbeat and vowing to 'get it done one day', Bateman left the tattoo parlour and joined me back at the subway station to return to our car. Boston may have been a disappointment for him, but for me it was the place where I had managed to successfully break the seventh law in a row. A run which I was sure would come to an end at some point. Even so, I was glad when we arrived at our motel in Sturbridge, where I couldn't wait to remove the ginger goatee which had sat on my face for the past few weeks. Drawing my shaver close to my face and peering into the mirror, suddenly I wasn't quite sure if I truly wanted to remove it. On the one hand it had helped me break fifteen laws out of a possible twenty-one, and had brought me to the startling level of seven successes in a row. On the other hand, it was ginger. Decision made. As the hairs washed away down the sink and out of my life, I studied my returning face in the mirror. I couldn't help but feel ever so slightly naked.

21

Two Men and a Tub

When man invented the bathtub, what was he trying to achieve? To make way for improvements and to deal with greater demand everything, over time, grows in size and stature to accommodate the needs of the people. It comes as no surprise to discover that the wing of a Boeing 747 is longer than the first ever flight nor that Lincoln Cathedral, for well over two hundred years the tallest building in the world, nowadays wouldn't make it into the top one thousand. So why, when everything else has grown to astronomical proportions, does the bathtub remain at – or even shrink to – a size where only certain parts of your body can be washed at a time? When the legs are in, the upper body is out, and when your chest is totally submerged your knees rise into the air and brave the generally arctic temperature of the bathroom. Surely some bright spark can create a bath which is seven feet long? That would accommodate most human life on earth and get back at the vertically challenged who must be feeling pretty smug about the entire bathtub crisis.

I put the question to Bateman as we pulled into Longmeadow, Massachusetts. Baths were on my mind simply because our arrival there marked the first time since adolescence that I had been glad tubs were the standard five feet. In Longmeadow it is illegal for two men to carry a bathtub across the village green, although it wasn't so much the carrying that I was concerned about. I knew I wasn't going to simply find one lying around, and if I had to borrow one I was going to need to transport it somehow. Suddenly, the modern bathtub's compact shape appealed to me for the very first time.

'OK, Bateman? We find the village green, get a bath-tub from somewhere, carry it over the green and we're done. It's a good job you're here. The law states two men.'

Although it was never going to be that easy, was it? No law was. However simple they appeared on paper, something would always happen to ruin the flow. In Spartanburg it was our inability to find the cemetery; the non-availability of kites almost scuppered me in Washington; and the fact that no girl wanted to miss out on the delights of Fontanelle for as long as five minutes meant certain failure there as well. My first impressions of Longmeadow did not inspire me with a great deal of hope. The village green was there all right but only a single shop could be seen. In a town of over 15,000 I knew there would be more than just the one retailer, but to have just the one around the town's focal point seemed very strange indeed. The shop, Spa On The Green, however, did sound rather encouraging in the bathtub stakes until I approached its front doors and realized it was in fact a doctor's surgery which offered organic skin care and body treatments, although from what I'm sure I saw printed in the window of the building, Dr Glen S. Brooks was a plastic surgeon. How very odd.

With no other shops in sight, Bateman and I headed across the green and strolled up the sidewalk. There was no doubt the green was picturesque in appearance, but it seemed oddly devoid of people. I needed to find a store where I could borrow a bathtub and so I needed a library to find one. Longmeadow, though, is a town where the buildings aren't readily identifiable from their looks. Other towns' buildings are easily recognized by pillars or clock towers, but not here. It's a town where the Town Hall is known as 'the building with the big white door' and the school is 'the building where all the kids are going', and neither has any other distinguishing features by which to tell them apart from the others. When we stopped the only person we saw, a small boy on his bike, and asked him where the library was, I wasn't surprised by his response: 'It's the big building at the end with the green windows.'

The Richard Salter Storrs Library, a big white building with the promised green windows, allowed me to use their Internet facilities and I browsed the on-line Longmeadow business directory. Under Home Improvements there were many painting and decorating services, my favourite being the cleverly named Odd Jobs at Odd Prices. None of them sounded as if they sold bathtubs or had any I could borrow. Under 'hardware – retail', however, there was one business that might be able to assist me.

We drove to Brightwood Hardware, a good mile from the lonely expanse of the town green. It stood in a tiny area of shops that was absolutely bursting with activity. One man was already in the hardware shop and a lady was loading some goods into the back of her car as a child rode past us both on his bike. Compared to the green, it was bursting with activity.

Although the gentleman who owned the store didn't sell bathtubs, he did know a place where I could drive to purchase one. After he had discovered that I wasn't from around the Longmeadow area and actually lived in the UK – to settle any kind of confusion I just said I was from London – he began to explain to me where I could find Baystate Plumbing and Heating Supply. After he had drawn me a rather indecipherable map, I thanked him for his time and, remembering that he had said something about an interstate, headed for the I-91.

Just north of Longmeadow, Baystate Plumbing and

Heating Supply was located in one of the twenty or so Springfields you can find throughout America. The store was one of those pleasant places where the products are laid out with special lighting and plastic fruit is used to enhance the environment. However, the Greek-style golden taps accenting the numerous bathtubs on display gave me a hint that this wasn't the type of shop which was going to simply allow me to borrow a tub for an hour.

'Can I help you, sir?' The voice came from behind an Elizabethan-style Jacuzzi, where a woman was seated at a desk filled with bathroom brochures.

'Um . . . yes. I was wondering if you had any' – what was the word? – 'smaller bathtubs? All the ones here seem to be too luxurious and grand for what I'm looking for.' Did that make any sense at all?

'Yes, of course, sir. If you would like to walk upstairs, there are plenty more up there.'

'Thanks.'

Now, thinking that I was going to have to purchase a bathtub, somehow get it into our car, and carry it across the town green before returning it for a full refund, I made my way upstairs to look for the smallest bathtub available. It certainly didn't help that our car was a saloon and wouldn't allow a bathtub of standard size easy access. The top level was nothing like the ground floor and looked like a well-lit attic. The laminate flooring which supported the tubs on the lower level was replaced here with plaster-board. And the bathtub hunt wasn't the greatest of successes. Either the tubs were too big or they were so outrageously overpriced that I didn't want to run the risk of paying for a bath I might not be able to get a refund on. In retrospect I should have asked the woman on the front desk if I could give her fifty dollars or so and have a tub delivered to the green where we could simply lift it off, carry it across the green, and then send it back. But at the time, I thought I had a much better idea.

'Hey, Bateman. There's bound to be some sort of scrap heap or tip nearby where people dispose of their old bathtubs. All we have to do is find it and bring one back to the green.'

'What?' Bateman asked before I rudely interrupted him with another wave of what I thought was pure genius.

'No, no, no. We drive around Longmeadow until we find a house that is being renovated or rebuilt or something. Hopefully they'll have a bathtub ready to install and we can just borrow it for an hour or so.'

As I write this now, I can't imagine what Bateman must have been thinking as he stood there, slightly slack-jawed, staring at me and the absurdity of my suggestion. Even a drive to the tip would still leave us with the problem of transporting the tub back to the green; the second idea was pure lunacy and Bateman was right to shake his head. Firstly, what were the chances that a house was being renovated nearby and that we had arrived on the very day that the builders were working on the bathroom? Furthermore, what builders in their right minds would allow two English strangers to borrow their bathtub 'for an hour or so'?

Maybe it was because I was desperately keen to secure an eighth consecutive victory or because with only two laws remaining after leaving Longmeadow I didn't want to end the spree the way I had begun it – with failure. Whatever, Bateman put his finger on it.

'That is the stupidest thing I've ever heard,' he said, not sure whether to laugh or seek some kind of medical assistance. 'Just give up.'

'No way, this is doable,' I shouted. 'I'm not letting it end like this,' I added, before coming out with a line I'm willing to bet has never before been voiced throughout the history of mankind: 'This is a bloody easy law; all I need is a bathtub!'

'Well, I saw a garage back there; I'm going to get a drink. Are you coming?'

As Bateman purchased a bottle of Gatorade, I picked up a pint of milk, then put it down again when I spotted something much more attractive through the window.

'Sod the milk, Bateman. I've got a far better idea.'

Outside was something I had only seen in cartoons and on television, yet was so typically American I was stunned that I hadn't ever seen one in all of my previous trips to the States. Just across the road, seated at a tiny table, was a kid selling lemonade. This cheered me up completely, just in time to take my mind off the bathtub fiasco. When I was growing up, a lemonade stall was the perennial image of how

American children who were too young to wait tables or too lazy for a paper round earned a quick buck. I dashed over to the stall in excitement and wasn't even disappointed when I discovered that the lemonade for sale was actually iced tea.

'How much is it?' I asked.

'Fifty cents a cup. How many would you like?'

'Just the one, please.'

When he had poured the remainder of the pitcher into my cup, I gave him a dollar and told him he could keep the change. Standing with my drink in hand and not wanting to down it in one for fear of throwing it all back up again, I decided it would be rude of me not to begin some sort of conversation.

'So how long have you been out here selling iced tea?' I asked.

'About three hours.'

'How much have you made?'

'About three dollars!' sniggered one of his friends behind him.

'Three dollars in three hours, hey? That's a dollar an hour. Not a bad hourly rate, that. Whatever you're saving up for I hope it's cheap,' I said. Mind you, he had positioned his stall outside a shop – good for potential customers but bad if they'd already purchased a drink.

'Well, I'm pretty sure I'm the only English customer you've had today,' I went on, knowing full well that the total of his takings meant he'd had four other customers all day and, if they were all as generous as me, really only two.

'I'm English, aren't I?' he replied in a thick American accent.

'I don't think so, buddy.'

'Well, I speak English. That makes me English, doesn't it?' He looked around at his friends to back him up.

'No. I'm English because I was born in England. You were born in America, which makes you American. It's not that difficult. Although all Americans emigrated from somewhere else. I might be able to tell you where your family came from. What's your surname?'

'Jeremy.'

'No, your second name.'

Not sure whether to reveal such vital information to a man who had openly admitted it was one of his dreams to buy lemonade from a kid on a lemonade stall, Jeremy kept his identity a secret and quite sensibly folded the legs of his table and prepared to make his way home with his friends.

'I feel nauseous and tired,' he said.

I wasn't surprised, after only five customers and an empty pitcher of iced tea; he had probably drunk most of the contents of the jug himself.

By the time I returned to our car, I had accepted that the law-breaking in Longmeadow was sadly not to be. I was out of zany schemes to pull a last-gasp success out of the bag and Bateman was running low on patience. I had at least fulfilled a lifelong ambition, and I had a few spare hours to prepare myself for what lay ahead. I only had a day in which to master the fine art, but as I made my way toward the village green where I should have been carrying a bathtub, I wisely used the time to practise walking on my hands.

22

Hands Up

It is a little-known fact that although California is the richest state in America, the state whose population has the greatest wealth is Connecticut. Unfortunately, the state is not rich in strange and obscure laws. In fact, if you ignore the regulation which decrees that throughout the state a pickle can only be considered to be a pickle if it bounces, there was just one ukase that I was looking forward to breaking.

In Hartford, Connecticut it is illegal to cross the road walking on your hands. Unfortunately, although I had been practising for the task the previous day in Longmeadow, I was still not proficient in the art. Originally I hadn't planned on breaking this law in a major city like Hartford, as I had read that the law pertained to the entire state, but then I saw a conflicting report which insisted that it applied only in the capital. Playing it safe, in case the law gods were watching, I found myself in the centre of Hartford on a slightly overcast Friday morning in search of the ideal place to cross the road.

It wasn't that early on a Friday morning, but still the streets of Hartford were strangely quiet. Very few cars were speeding by, and just a handful of pedestrians were walking past the countless shops, many of which were closed.

'Where do you wanna do this, then?' asked Bateman.

'Well, this is the state capital. May as well do it at the capitol building.'

Overlooking the city's 41-acre Bushnell Park, the Connecticut State Capitol building was exceptionally beautiful and looked like a Scottish castle with a Vatican-style dome charging up into the sky. We really had saved the best till last.

I'd never actually been inside a state capitol and, with Hartford's being the last we'd see, decided it was about time I did. The wooden carved pillars and chandeliers that hung from the towering ceilings looked absolutely stunning from behind the glass doors – which were firmly locked.

'Never mind,' I said to Bateman. 'I came here to cross the road on my hands anyway.'

As I walked away from the capitol's steps and down toward the park I could hear a man's voice offering advice as to how I could get into the building. Too far away to care I simply shouted my gratitude and shrugged my shoulders. I didn't need the state capitol; I could already see the place where the road-crossing was going to take place.

The Soldiers and Sailors Memorial Arch stood in the centre of Bushnell Park just yards from Hartford's historic carousel, which, like most things in the city, was empty. The last time I had seen a monument dedicated to the soldiers and sailors of a particular state it was in Indianapolis and came with the added bonus of a roundabout. This tremendous arch was dedicated to the four thousand Hartford soldiers who fought in the civil war, four hundred of whom lost their lives whilst fighting for the Union. The structure, 116 feet in height, is made of terracotta from Boston and brownstone from nearby Portland, and the arch stands between two towers like the entrance to some medieval fortress. On each tower eight-foot-tall statues depict the kinds of men who left their homes to fight. What impressed me most of all was the fact that the arch was too narrow for two lanes of traffic to pass through so a one-way system had been enforced, surely making the width of road quite easily hand-walkable (and if that isn't a word, it should be).

Walking on your hands isn't as easy as it seems, and if you are equipped with similar balance skills to mine it's nigh on impossible. The trick I'd learned in Longmeadow was to straighten the legs and allow them to lean slightly in front. Too little and you were back on your feet, too much and you had an imminent date with the concrete below. After six or seven failed attempts during which the furthest I travelled was two steps of the hands, or about three feet – which, put in easier, more digestible terms, was nowhere near far enough – it was time I thought about the crossing more carefully. As I stood back and pondered how success might be achieved, the small crowd who had been attracted by my antics waited patiently to see my next failed attempt.

'We'll cheat.'

Bateman was startled. 'What? How can we cheat?'

'Well, not cheat exactly. I'm still going to walk on my hands, it's just that you're going to assist me.'

'How?'

'I'm gonna put my feet up on your shoulders and I'll walk on my hands that way. It's like a boxer being helped out of the ring. The trainers let him lean on them but he's still doing the walking, isn't he?'

Bateman agreed to my tenuous idea, and took the wallet and loose change I handed him from my pockets. Then he grasped my ankles.

And so it was that, looking like two grown-up kids taking part in a very lonesome wheelbarrow race at a school sports day, Bateman lifted my legs onto his shoulders and supported me as I scurried across the road on my hands. Standing up on the other side, I tucked my shirt into my shorts and awaited the congratulation of the crowd. After numerous attempts I had finally managed to complete the challenge and surely I was due some adulation from the people who had cheered me on when I was going it alone. But everyone seemed to turn away and return to whatever it was they were doing before they had been attracted to the Memorial Arch. I don't think Americans look too kindly on blatant cheating.

Having met one of them face to face in Chicago and having heard two children discuss their love for them at San Francisco airport earlier in the trip, Bateman and I wanted to delve deeper into the one culture, other than America's penchant for bizarre laws, which separates our two nations more than any other – America's obsession with guns. With the end of the spree being only a trip to New Jersey, a monkey and a cigarette away, we tore a page out of the Hartford Yellow Pages and made our way to the outskirts of the city to see if it was possible for us to use a real gun with live ammunition. Connecticut, whose Gun Code of 1650 reads: 'All men shall bear arms, and every male person shall have in continual readiness a good musket or other gun, fit for service,' seemed the perfect place.

Wolf's Indoor Range and Shooting Center is a rather daunting place to enter if you're British and used to think AK47 was a pop group. Its proprietor, Ray Sausanavitch, however, is anything but intimidating, and cordially invited us into his shop. 'What can I do for you, guys?'

'We're from England and we were just wondering if it was at all possible to experience shooting a gun?'

Ray looked regretful and shook his head. 'Sorry,

guys. You have to have a licence, I'm afraid. Some people from the UK shot here a month or two ago but they knew someone who did have a licence and so he signed them in.'

'Oh, OK. Thanks anyway. We'll just look round, if that's OK?'

Ray, obviously not wanting to disappoint us and with a similar philosophy to that of a game-show host who is determined that no one shall leave empty-handed, offered us a chance to at least see people shooting and took us into a viewing area where we stood behind bullet-proof glass and watched a gentleman shooting at a kind of target I had never seen before. On the piece of squared paper were sixteen circles that created a spiral which decreased in size the closer to the centre they were and was rather more interesting than the pictures of swagbag-wielding criminals I was expecting. After the man had offloaded his first two rounds and hit a perfect twelve, he noticed that we had been watching every bullet he fired. As he pulled the target sheet down from its hanger and made his way out of the range to join us in the viewing area, the man, who was in his fifties with short grey hair, looked less like a marksman and more like a university English professor.

Barry Leeds, a university English professor and part-time shooting instructor, removed his ear defenders and introduced himself. Bateman and I did likewise but it didn't seem to make the slightest bit of difference as Barry called me Peter twice in as many minutes. After apologizing profusely, he explained that his friend Peter should be meeting him shortly and that was where the confusion lay. Until Peter arrived, it appeared I would have to be his temporary replacement.

'So are you guys shooting?' he asked.

'No. We need someone to sign us in, apparently,' I replied, using the heaviest hint I could muster without actually winking slyly and nudging my elbow into his stomach.

After returning to the range to hit fifteen out of the sixteen circles, missing the final one, which I was sure a bullet couldn't even fit, by a considerable margin, Barry led us into the shop, where I discovered that members could try any gun they wanted, from Colt 22s, Glock 36s and Beretta 92 SFs to other guns I'd never heard of before, for only ten dollars an hour. Ray took Barry to one side and clearly asked him something, pointing in our direction. A simple nod of Barry's head later, our names were signed in and we were ready to shoot. With Ray's generosity growing by the minute, we only needed to cover the cost of the bullets.

'Right, I can only take you into the range one at a time so one of you will have to wait in the viewing area,' Barry explained. 'Who's going first? Luke or Peter?'

'Rich,' I corrected.

'Sorry, Rich.'

'Bateman, you can go first, mate.'

As Barry took Bateman into the range I was joined in the viewing area by Barry's friend Peter Marino whom I welcomed enthusiastically, seeing the end of my Peter duties in sight, and we got talking about guns and the police's need for them.

'I hear all cops in England have a gun now,' he said.

'No. Where did you hear that? It's really not like here. Apart from at airports, the police aren't usually armed. All they need is a truncheon.'

'Really?'

'Yeah. No one needs them because no one seems to have guns. Over here, the guns are out and the only way to combat them is with more guns. I met one in Chicago, actually, when I was stopped by the cops.'

Bateman, who had earlier bragged that he would be much better than me owing to his experience with an air rifle when he was younger, hadn't done too badly apart from the fact that on his target, which was arranged like an archery target, every single one of his twelve shots had drifted to the right-hand side. It was time for me to enter the range and fire off a few rounds.

As soon as the door opened and I entered the shooting range for the first time, the smell of cordite filled me with instant concern about what I was doing. The range rules which adorned the concrete walls behind the fifteen firing ports didn't do much to ease my anxiety either. 'Rapid firing', 'quick draw', 'hip-shooting' and 'hammering the fan' were all banned, and with my zero understanding of the world of guns, for all I knew I could have been doing one of those just by standing still.

Barry chaperoned me into port thirteen and handed me his gun. He taught me how to hold it before explaining to me the two different styles of firing.

'Now there's the single action and the double action,' he said. 'One way you cock the gun yourself and the other you don't.'

'Right,' I replied, congratulating myself for not sniggering at the word 'cock'.

'Have you ever fired a gun before?' he asked.

'Only once, at a fair. It was an air rifle and I accidentally held it by my face. When I pulled the trigger the recoil almost broke my jaw.'

'In that case we'll use the single action, which means you pull the hammer back yourself before firing. That way you get a more accurate shot.'

'OK.'

'Right, load your gun and you're ready to shoot.'

Just for the record I loaded .38 Special cartridges into a 6-inch Ruger Model GP100 .357 Magnum which to my English ears sounded more like an Ordnance Survey map grid reference than the description of a firearm.

Lifting the gun tentatively with both hands and staring at the target thirty feet away from where I was standing, I cocked the gun with the thumb of my right hand. By now both hands were shaking and sweating.

'How do you feel?' Barry asked.

'My hands are shaking. I can't aim very well.'

'They're shaking because you're excited.'

'I don't think it's excitement that's making them do it. They did this in Chicago and I certainly wasn't excited then.'

Closing an eye and gripping slightly harder on the gun, I released the first of my bullets, penetrating the target to score a seven.

'Good shot!' said Barry as I turned round and almost pointed the gun at him. 'Just ease off the grip slightly.'

After the first round of twelve bullets, Barry brought the target back in and it appeared I had hit four nines and a couple of tens.

'Not bad, hey?' I asked.

'Not bad, not bad at all.'

A second target was placed on the mechanical pulleys and jerked back to thirty feet. By now I felt totally at ease with a loaded firearm and with the remaining thirteen bullets I managed to hit the ten another five times and the nine another four.

'That was really good,' said Barry as we entered the viewing area, where Bateman had just learned from Peter that he was something called 'left eye dominant' and that was why he had sent all his shots to the right.

Back in the shop, I explained why I was really in America and assured Barry that there would be no way his students would ever study a book I wrote, and would probably find a better use for it as toilet paper. Barry, it turned out, was the vice president of the Norman Mailer Society and had published two books he had written about the novelist. On cue, Ray turned to a shelf behind him and produced a copy of *The Enduring Vision of Norman Mailer* by Barry H. Leeds as if they had rehearsed the presentation several times before.

By now, Ray's cousin Dave Zienka had joined us in the shop and Ray's young nephew Mark was studying a five-pound note and some British coins Bateman had accidentally spilled while looking for money to pay for the bullets we had used. As Mark collected foreign coins, Bateman and I attempted to present him with an example of every British one, unfortunately falling short having failed to find a twenty pence or a two-pound coin. Promising to post the two coins to Mark when we returned to the UK, I began to question America's coin system and praised the British one as the simplest to understand in the world.

'Why do you think they're better, Rich?' asked Barry.

'Look, I'll show you.' I laid the coins we had just given to Mark out on the counter. 'For starters, the American five cents is bigger than the ten-cent coin. Why?'

'Oh yeah. I've never thought about that.'

'In Britain we use the bronze, silver, gold method which everyone understands. Look: small bronze, big bronze, small silver, big silver, small weird-shaped silver, big weird-shaped silver and then gold. All in order of value. Simple.'

'I see what you mean.'

In yet another generous act, and in return for the coins we had given his nephew, Ray presented us with a Wolf's Shooting Range key ring and medallion and a golden dollar coin each – the latter being seldom used due to the fact that they were in circulation with the silver dollar coin which was similar in appearance and size to the quarter. It proved my earlier point about the confusion caused by the American monetary system perfectly.

'It's illegal to have wire cutters in your glove box in El Paso, Texas,' said Dave, who until now had only spoken to introduce himself.

'Is it?' I replied. 'I decided to keep well clear of Texas mainly because they still have the death penalty. I haven't been to Florida either for the same reason.'

'Yeah, cos of the immigrants breaking through the fences. If you were caught with wire cutters, they'd presume you were helping illegals into the country and then you'd be in trouble.'

When Barry and Peter left it seemed as if it was time we should be leaving too, and we shook everyone's hand and wished them our best. For only the price of the bullets (twelve dollars in all) we had received the guidance of a qualified instructor, been handed a souvenir key ring and medallion and even been re-imbursed two whole golden dollars. Not a bad day. Not a bad day at all. To my eyes, guns were still a scourge of society, but the people behind the triggers definitely weren't, and if the people I had met in the shooting range that day were typical of gun owners across America, I felt safe in the knowledge that maybe the country wasn't in such a trigger-happy state as we have been led to believe.

The Connecticut Grand Hotel and Conference Center fit perfectly into that sector of cheap hotels which attempt to pass as five-star accommodation. The kind of place I love. Using my discount coupon book for the umpteenth time on the trip so far, I managed to secure a room for only $66 (£36). Most rooms overlooked the inside courtyard, which boasts fountains and exotic plants, and we were free to make full use of the pool, gym, sauna and spa facilities. Just for that certain touch of extravagance, the hotel boasts a magnificent ballroom as well. But that evening Bateman and I found ourselves in the restaurant propping up the bar where the television was tuned to *Family Feud*, the American version of *Family Fortunes*, and being constantly entertained by the answers given by the contestants – who get a round of applause after every answer, however daft and inconceivable.

'Name a fruit that's messy to eat.'

'Chocolate.'

Classic.

23

Start Spreading the News

I was surprised by New Jersey. Until now I'd always considered the state to be one big suburb of New York where all the city's workers commuted to and from each day, and that the name 'the Garden State' was selected for its ironic qualities. The Bear Mountain Bridge was the longest suspension bridge in the world when construction was completed in 1924, but today it stands as a testament to time and still looks as new as ever. The height of the bridge coupled with the deep and sheer elevation and gradient of the banks which fall perilously into the Hudson River makes the view stupendous. The different trees which line the banks present a patchwork quilt of natural technicolour which seems to find new and exciting shades to blend into to amaze the viewer. The Hudson below, after one final change of direction, begins its direct and lineal progression through the state until its approach into New York where it flows alongside Manhattan tower blocks before washing into the Atlantic. Quite apart from the fact that the toll is only to be paid by traffic travelling in the opposite direction, I'm further cheered by what's waiting for us on the river's opposite bank, immediately at the bridge's end. Not surrounded by traffic as in Long Beach, used improperly as in Indianapolis or serving no great purpose like the two I'd seen in Salt Lake City, stood the winner of *America's Greatest Roundabout*. Set in deep woodland and offering four exits, it was bound to be the eventual winner. The fifth one of its kind in ten thousand or more miles and I was sure it was to be the last . . . until we saw another a mile further down the road – one that could maybe push the earlier contender into silver position.

As August was drawing to a close so was the crime spree, and the law in New Jersey seemed the perfect one on which to end it all. Throughout the state it is illegal to feed whisky or offer cigarettes to monkeys at a zoo. Possessing no spirits and having a smoker as my travel partner, I'm not offering any prizes for guessing which of the two products I was going to proffer to the apes.

Sticking to a timberland road which passed almost no homes other than farms before reaching a park with enough play and sports equipment to satisfy a metropolis's children, we finally arrived at the only zoo we could find within fifty miles of our motel which definitely stated that monkeys were a part of their attraction. After the formality of paying the entrance fee, I was handed a map of the zoo and discovered, to my relief, that the monkeys were to be found in the exact centre of the park as if they were the jewel in the crown of the zoo.

As we had no great sense of urgency about the task ahead, Bateman and I decided to do a lap of the zoo to ascertain how difficult the law would be to break. No sooner had I passed through the entrance than I was confronted by the cage of a Syrian brown bear, a sign which asked you to not feed the animal, and an American and his daughter who were doing just that.

Just so you know, the Syrian brown bear is closely related to the grizzly and is the smallest subspecies of brown bear. While it sat upright with its legs out in front of the rest of its body I discovered that this particular species feeds on plant parts and small mammals and definitely wasn't partial to the 'cool original' flavour Doritos which were being hurled over the top of its cage by the girl and her father. Turning away in disappointment that people would want to offer such things to an animal when the sign strictly asked them not to – rather hypocritical of me – I made my way further into the park.

On the opposite side from the bears, the wildfowl lake was home to flamingos, otters, swans and, bizarrely, a cow, which stood at the top of a tiny steep bank trying her hardest not to slip into the water. I was looking forward to seeing the aoudads (an animal

I'd never heard of) but was disappointed when I discovered it was a North African sheep. The wolves were doing their very best job of hiding in the undergrowth, and I couldn't feed the goats because many of the bird seed dispensers were broken. I felt it was time to lay everything on the line.

'Right, that's it. Let's do this, Bateman. I'm gonna need some sort of branch and no people around.'

I needed a branch because there was a second fence surrounding the cage that the monkeys called home, which added about six feet to the space between you and any primate you finally came face to face with.

Now, I know that offering a cigarette to a monkey is bad in itself. I'm sure whisky would be worse but I agree that a cigarette is not an ideal item to let a monkey get his hands on. But if you've visited Longleat or a similar safari park and experienced the amount of damage a group of apes can do to your car, you do begin to lose sympathy with the furry vandals.

'Right, I'm gonna attach the cigarette to the end of the stick and poke it through the bars until a monkey takes it from me. OK?' I asked Bateman, just to check that the plan sounded as foolproof as I hoped.

'Right.' He seemed convinced enough.

Maybe the end of the stick wasn't sufficiently pointed and couldn't pierce the cigarette properly, or maybe I was too eager to put an end to the escapade, but the plan didn't work and the cigarette dropped into the area between fence and cage.

'Stuff it.'

Nobody was looking. I leaped the fence and approached the cage, and was met by half a dozen Rhesus monkeys who hissed and jeered my approach. Jumping and stomping angrily on the floor, they danced in rage as I quickly picked the cigarette off the ground and threw it into their cage. It had been done. The cigarette had been offered and I had completed the spree. I wanted to shout for joy and broadcast my achievements to the world, but all I felt capable of doing was slumping by the side of the fence and breathing a deep sigh of relief. I couldn't even do that for fear of being dragged into the cage by the monkeys.

When I jumped back over the fence and turned round to check that the monkey hadn't choked on the tobacco, I noticed that I needn't have worried. The Rhesus monkey, the sign informed me, came from southern Asia and northern China, and fed on nuts, berries, grains, insects and plants. Tobacco, remember, is a plant.

And so that was it. No fireworks, no tickertape parade or celebration of any kind greeted the completion of the spree – just the distant noise of the animals which surrounded me. Sure I was happy it was over, but I should have planned ahead and at least brought a party popper into the zoo with me. Bateman, though, had a better plan.

After over eleven thousand miles of travel, staying in motels ranging from the abysmal to the moderately

OK, Bateman knew what we more than certainly deserved. Why shouldn't we combine our credit cards? Why couldn't we stay in the only five-star waterfront hotel in New York City? Stuff it. That night, the celebrations would be held in Battery Park, overlooking the Statue of Liberty in our own 500-dollar room at the Ritz!

After a pleasant discussion about Bolton Wanderers and their hopes for a successful Premiership campaign, our taxi driver dropped us off at the steps of the Ritz where our bags were taken from us, the door was opened by one of the helpful doormen and we probably became the first people in Ritz-Carlton history to check in in shorts and T-shirts with crates of Budweiser resting on our shoulders and a motel coupon book which brought about no reduction whatsoever in the price.

Leo, a concierge who was clearly accustomed to being tipped by the wealthy, showed us round our room and received two dollars for his pains. The clean and superbly presented room, which had a fantastic view of Brooklyn Bridge, Battery Park and the Statue of Liberty, came with a telescope through which the landmarks synonymous with the Big Apple could be viewed in closer detail.

When we had taken some time to empty the fridge of the entire contents of the mini-bar and replace them with thirty-six cans of Budweiser (I know how much a mini-bar costs and I'm not falling for that game), Bateman emerged from the bathroom dressed in a white Ritz-Carlton dressing gown at a little after three in the afternoon.

'Right, that's me sorted. I'm getting my money's worth and staying here until a minute before check-out time.'

'They've got robes?' I asked in surprise.

'Yeah. There's another one in there.'

Excitedly I ran to the bathroom and slipped into my very own dressing gown and joined Bateman at the window of our room where, with the goddess of liberty as our witness, we chinked our lager-filled champagne glasses and congratulated ourselves on successfully completing seventeen laws out of a possible twenty-four.

But it's never that simple, is it? Twenty-four is a terrible number on which to end. It has no rounded qualities and sounds as if things are not quite complete. I'm pretty sure God only added 'thou shalt not desire your neighbour's house' or whatever it is because he wanted to make the commandments up to a nice round number instead of leaving them at nine. And Ali Baba probably hired his useless cousin just so he could have forty thieves. Apart from the fact that it is illegal to walk down the street whilst reading a book, New York City didn't provide anything in the way of interesting laws and Bateman and I were left wondering how a twenty-fifth could possibly be broken before my flight the following day.

During an evening drink at the Ritz's exclusive bar,

Rise, on the fourteenth floor of the hotel, paying twelve dollars for a cocktail where I could hardly taste the alcohol, we enjoyed fantastic night-time views of the New York and New Jersey skylines and the Brooklyn and Manhattan bridges beneath which tourist boats illuminated the Hudson River far below.

The following morning Bateman was out of bed surprisingly early, making full use of his remaining time in the hotel. Still in the gown he had slept in, he was whirling round the bathroom like a man possessed.

'Rich, do you want a towel to take home?'

'Yeah. I was gonna take one of the hand towels.'

'Right then, I'll nick the other four.'

Returning from the room with the towels and a wash bag, Bateman began rummaging through drawers and cupboards, taking everything he could find which carried the Ritz-Carlton motif and stuffing it into his bag. A shoe horn, a stationery kit, pens, envelopes, four of the leather cases in which the hotel kept their menus, and anything else which caught his eye seemed to make its way into Bateman's luggage. I was sure that if our room hadn't been located on the tenth floor, Bateman would have had a go at anything that wasn't bolted down. He had even managed to swipe a leather notelet holder which he had found outside our room by the lift.

'That looks nice. Can't I have it?' I asked, after poking my head round the corner of our door to see if it had been replaced.

'No, it's mine. Just go down a few floors and steal one of theirs,' he replied.

However, with chambermaids watching my every move, I returned to our room empty-handed just as Bateman put the finishing touches to his own personal crime spree, stopping short at the television.

'Are you sure you don't want the carpet, Bateman?'

'No, I'm quite happy with what I have, thanks.'

As we packed the remainder of our belongings – and the hotel's – into our bags and began to make our way towards the lift, I noticed the receipt which had been pushed under our door during the night. Day of checkout: August 30. August the 30th. It had been exactly a month since Bateman had received his speeding fine, and today a warrant for his arrest would be issued in the state of Wyoming. If the fact that his luggage had doubled in weight since we arrived at the Ritz wasn't a criminal offence, his jump of bail certainly was and we had the piece of paper to prove it.

'Hey. That judge is waiting for you to show up in Wyoming, mate. That's twenty-five laws. Twenty-six if you're caught by security,' I yelled.

'Really? I suppose that's it then. It's over.'

As we stood by the lift to take us out of my last hotel it seemed like a lifetime ago that we had checked into the first one, in San Francisco, with so many miles to travel and so little idea of what was going to happen. I couldn't wait to get home and see family and friends once more but for that brief instant in the corridor of the Ritz I wanted to do it all over again – meet the same people, see the same places and break the same laws – though possibly with the added excitement of being successful at more than seventeen. There was no great surge of jubilation, but I felt a strange sense of pride in what I had achieved. I would have suggested a final celebration with Bateman in the way we both would have liked to remember the end of a fantastic summer ... but there was only one Hooters in Manhattan and it was too far away.

When the lift finally reached us, illuminating the down arrow and pinging to announce its arrival, I was about to step inside when Bateman swung his arm across my chest and pointed at the desk.

'Look! There's another leather note holder there, mate. Nick it.'

Epilogue

Bateman still owns the summons he was presented with on the day of his speeding offence and as far as I know it is currently hanging in a frame on a wall in his house. The state of Wyoming did nothing to detain him in the country and he eventually left the States earlier than expected, a little short of two weeks after me, having had his money and credit cards stolen in a Miami nightclub, sitting at a 200-dollar VIP table.

The roadkill game, which Bateman would have considered a personal triumph, is still without a winner due to the fact that an adequate and fair scoring system has yet to be adopted.

The only one of Brenda's premonitions to be realized was that I moved house.

We await the bill from the Ritz-Carlton for our souvenirs.

Acknowledgements

There are many people whom I would like to thank for making everything possible, not least my agent, Rebecca Winfield, and my publishing team who believed in me and actually thought I could write a good book in under two months. I wrote *a* book, at least.

Before anyone else I'd like to thank my neighbour Lewis and his family for luring me out of the pub and inviting me to take part in their yearly game of Balderdash which instilled the crazy idea in my head in the first place. I'd also like to express my gratitude to David Green of the *West Briton* for letting me write the story and to potential Pulitzer Prize winner Chris Mardith for being a perfect anagram of my name.

Special thanks should go to Arden Deloris for helping to kick-start my campaign when it seemed nothing was going my way. Despite his snap victory, caused by the most definite bout of beginner's luck,

I'm just relieved and appreciative that Arden was kind and approachable enough to take me seriously.

Thanks to Joye for sharing a 'pint' with Bateman and me, and to her mother for making sure I use my country facts more wisely in the future, and to Ann Traczek for correctly referring to soccer as football and for sticking up for me in a recent on-line forum when, for some strange reason, I was the subject.

I'm grateful for the welcome Bateman and I received from all the residents of Mineral Point, especially Joy Gieseke, Carole and Norman Rule and Catherine Whitford who were overwhelmingly helpful and responded with unstinting generosity, and exceptionally thankful for Lee and Jen's hospitality and cordial reception of the news that they would be welcoming us into their home for two days longer than I had originally planned.

For not shooting me in the face and instead very helpfully directing us back to the interstate, I'd like to thank the bullet-proof-clad police force of Chicago; and many thanks to Bill Stover and his son David who, like Arden, weren't initially shocked by my request and did all they could to make the law-breaking possible.

I'd like to express great appreciation to Raymond Sausanavitch, his nephew Mark and all the staff at Wolf's Indoor Range and Shooting Center for allowing me to fire a gun for the first time, and to Barry Leeds and his friend Peter Marino whose instruction and assistance were invaluable.

Support at home was provided by my good friends Jon Davey, Matt Reed, Ian Parsonage, Sam Savage, my girlfriend Becky Brown, Kirstin Prisk, Tim Rice and his interested pupils, and Tony Parker, whose constant requests for pints have been the only bane in the writing, and to Sue, Mick, Tony and Carl Reynolds who will be among the very few people to have actually bought the book. And to Becky Watts, Mike Dennis and Mikey Underhill who really didn't do a thing but wanted their names mentioned in the prose.

Obviously I would like to thank Bateman for accompanying me on such a bizarre escapade and for never questioning the reasoning behind why he doesn't just refuse. Bateman, I'm sure, would like to take this opportunity to thank all the Hooters girls, especially Samantha, and Halifax credit cards who have sponsored him financially and will no doubt leave him in economic oblivion.

My thanks go to Dave O'Brien for inviting me so warmly onto Indianapolis's airwaves and to his co-host Ed Wank for his similar hospitality and for having a funny name, and to Angela Walker for being good-looking enough for Bateman to be smitten by her beauty, presenting me with the chance to have a good laugh at his expense.

And to the proprietor of the only bar in Ocean City who had the good sense to accept our driving licences and allow us to drink in his bar.

No doubt I have unwittingly forgotten to thank numerous people and for that I apologize. There was no deliberate intention to exclude people and if anyone feels left out it has been through a fault of *my* own.

Lastly I would like to thank my brother Craig and my parents for their love and support and for letting me do such crazy things.

I FOUGHT THE LAW
by Dan Kieran

It seems that the British way of life is being eroded at every turn.
But despite what we're led to believe, it's not being attacked by an
increase in immigration, or a glut of asylum seekers. No, our
adversary is a distinctly un-British addiction to over-work and over-
consumption and the meaningless toil that has begun to interfere
with our daily lives. Add to that a climate of terror that has
endangered any rational enquiry and you can't help but begin to
wonder what's happened to our great British democracy?

In an attempt to raise our flagging spirits – and to find out exactly
what's going wrong in 21st century Britain – Dan Kieran enlisted the
help of an unlikely band of eccentrics who are fighting back. As Dan
explains why the path to Britain's future prosperity involves you
quitting your job and spending much more time down the pub,
follow his adventures as he . . .

- *Joins a group of protestors – five of whom were arrested for eating cakes
  in Parliament Square – to discover how New Labour have been taking
  liberties with our liberties.*
- *Spends an afternoon on the roof of a bus station in Derby with an
  unlikely protestor called Dorothy.*
- *Encounters the pensioners who let off stink bombs in court in order to
  force an extension to a public enquiry – and won their case.*
- *Meets a man who dresses like Chaplin's tramp and keeps getting arrested
  outside Downing Street – because we no longer have the right to remain
  silent either.*
- *Finds King Arthur alive and well and up a tree – thrashing at the police
  with his sword!*
- *Reveals why a flat-pack chest of drawers from one well-known store is
  more likely to kill you than a suicide bomber . . . and – in this so-called
  ASBO nation of ours . . .*
- *why one woman got an ASBO for being naked in her own home and a
  Tourettes sufferer was given an ASBO for swearing.*

So, whether it's fighting to protect our environment, our freedom, or
the right to live in an unconventional way, *I Fought the Law* is a
celebration of the British spirit, and a call to arms for all those for
whom enough is enough!

9780593058084

NOW AVAILABLE FROM BANTAM PRESS

BANTAM PRESS

THE UNDERDOG
One man's odyssey through the
world's wackiest competitions
by Joshua Davis

Joshua Davis had a dream. He dreamt of being the best. It didn't really matter what he was the best at, he just wanted to be number one, the big enchilada, to say that he had made it. This is how it began: Josh was driving through the Mojave Desert one day when he saw a sign for the American arm-wrestling championship – all comers welcome. He decided to enter. He came fourth, out of four, but this was enough to secure him a place on Team USA and the chance of a show-down with the 'Russian Ripper' at the world championships in Poland (that didn't end very well either).

But Josh had tasted the dizzy rush of competition and wanted more. And more turned out to be the most outlandish contests in the world – from bull fighting in Spain and backward running in Italy, to sumo wrestling and the World Sauna Championship in Sweden.

Joshua's quest is by turns hilarious, harrowing and a little insane, but it is also inspiring – because, after all, every underdog deserves his day.

'Extremely funny'
Daily Telegraph

'Davis embodies the unique idiocy that made America great . . . deeply personal, post-modern, manifest destiny for the *Jackass* generation'
Mil Millington, author of *Things My Girlfriend and I Argue About*

9780552154390

CORGI BOOKS